Nelson Mandela

FRONT-PAGE LIVES

Nelson Mandela

Patrick Catel

www.raintreepublishers.co.uk
Visit our website to find out more information about Raintree books.

To order:
☎ Phone 0845 6044371
📄 Fax +44 (0) 1865 312263
📧 Email myorders@raintreepublishers.co.uk

Customers from outside the UK please telephone +44 1865 312262

Raintree is an imprint of Capstone Global Library Limited, a company incorporated in England and Wales having its registered office at 7 Pilgrim Street, London, EC4V 6LB – Registered company number: 6695582

Text © Capstone Global Library Limited 2010
First published in hardback in 2010
Paperback edition first published in 2011

The moral rights of the proprietor have been asserted.

Edited by Adam Miller, Andrew Farrow, and Adrian Vigliano
Designed by Kim Miracle
Original illustrations © Capstone Global Library, LLC
Illustrated by Mapping Specialists
Picture research by Ruth Blair
Originated by Steve Walker
Printed in China by CTPS

ISBN 978 0 431115 81 8 (hardback)
13 12 11 10 09
10 9 8 7 6 5 4 3 2 1

ISBN 978 0 431115 87 0 (paperback)
14 13 12 11 10
10 9 8 7 6 5 4 3 2 1

British Library Cataloguing in Publication Data
Catel, Patrick.
   Nelson Mandela. -- (Front page lives)
968'.06'092-dc22

A full catalogue record for this book is available from the British Library.

Acknowledgements
We would like to thank the following for permission to reproduce photographs: Alamy/© Alexander Caminada p. **69**; Art Archive/Private Collection MD p. **10**; Corbis/Bernard Bisson/Sygma p. **63**; Corbis/Bettmann p. **31**; Corbis/Bettmann p. **56**; Corbis/Bob Adelman p. **44**; Corbis/David Brauchli/Sygma p. **73**; Corbis/David Turnley p. **61**; Corbis/International Defence and Aid Fund/Handout/Reuters p. **41**; Corbis/Jon Jones/Sygma p. **7**; Corbis/REUTERS/Richard Chung p. **74**; Corbis/Rick Friedman p. **87**; Getty Images/AFP/JEAN-PIERRE MULLER p. **79**; Getty Images/Hulton Archive p. **29**; Rex Features/Dennis Stone p. **89**; Rex Features/Peter Heimsath p. **82**; Rex Features/Richard Young p. **93**; Rex Features/Sipa Press p. **18**; Rex Features/Sutton-Hibbert p. **53**; Shutterstock background images and design features throughout.

Cover photograph of Nelson Mandela casting his vote at the ballot box on election day, 1994 reproduced with permission of Corbis/Peter Turnley.

Every effort has been made to contact copyright holders of material reproduced in this book. Any omissions will be rectified in subsequent printings if notice is given to the publishers.

Contents

Some words are shown in bold, **like this**. You can find out what they mean by looking in the glossary.

Leader of a rainbow nation

On 10 May 1994, Nelson Mandela addressed the world as the new president of South Africa. It was an amazing accomplishment after having spent much of his adult life in prison for resisting a racist government. His election to the office of president signalled the future of a new South Africa, where all people were represented and free, no matter what their skin colour.

HISTORY UNFOLDING

In 1994, South Africa was coming out of many years of suffering under **apartheid**. In the apartheid system, people were classified according to crude racial categories such as black, white, or coloured (people of mixed race). Under this system, people from non-white categories were not allowed to vote. The election of 1994 was historic because it was the first time ever that black and coloured people in South Africa were given the right to vote. This caused a lot of tension. There were many people who were against the end of apartheid. They felt that the only way different races could live in harmony was through separation. People protested on both sides of the issue, often violently.

People around the world and in South Africa waited anxiously as events unfolded. This was a time of major transition, and the country of South Africa had been through many months and years of violence leading up to this moment in history. Not all was calm beforehand. In the days leading up to the election, there were bombings in some cities of

*Nelson Mandela celebrates his election victory. His **inauguration** to the office of president ended more than three centuries of white rule in South Africa.*

South Africa. In one bomb attack in downtown Johannesburg, a large South African city, at least 9 people were killed and 92 people were injured. The very next day, two more bombs went off. One, in the city of Germiston, killed 10 people and injured 41 people. In Pretoria 2 people were killed and 30 were injured. It was suspected that the bombs had been planted in attempts to scare black people away from voting.

1994 ELECTION

However, after waiting so long to gain the right to vote, people could not be kept away. Very early in the morning on 27 April 1994, millions of people in South Africa began lining up to cast their votes in the historic election. The whole world was watching intently, fearing bloodshed. Instead of violence, however, they saw a peaceful election. No bombs went off during the three days of voting. Some people had to wait in line for hours, and there were some reports of voting problems. However, it was a peaceful day for the country of South Africa.

> *"The time for healing the wounds has come... The time to build is upon us."*
> —Nelson Mandela

Though voting went smoothly in cities, there were some problems in **rural** areas. In those areas, some people had to walk for days to reach a polling place, where votes are cast during an election. Some ballot boxes arrived late, which delayed the opening of polling places for days. Voters had to wait, some sleeping in fields, but they would not be kept from casting their ballots.

In cities, long queues formed, made up of black and white people standing together. This was a sight never before seen in South Africa. Apartheid had controlled the movements of black people, and there were laws that had forbidden them from crossing into white areas. Those laws were no longer in effect, and all people could cast their votes together. One black man who went into a white area to vote to avoid a long queue said "This is 100 percent better, for sure." A white man who waited in line for 7 hours said "A change is coming in this land, and it will be a good change and I'm all for it."[1]

MANDELA'S INAUGURATION

The inauguration of Mandela was an exciting celebration held in Pretoria, one of the three capital cities of South Africa. The election of 1994 was the first time in South African history that black people were allowed to cast votes. Throughout the country's history, native African people had been persecuted and victimized by the white people who had landed on their shores. The fact that the election ended in the way native Africans wanted was cause for much celebration. Thousands of South Africans crowded the lawn outside the government buildings, and all

Frederik Willem de Klerk (1936–)

As president before Mandela, F. W. de Klerk played a part in making Mandela's election possible.

Born in Johannesburg in 1936, de Klerk served in several cabinet positions under President P. W. Botha, and succeeded him as leader of the National Party in 1989. De Klerk was then elected president and soon announced his historic policy of reform, freed Mandela, and began dismantling apartheid.

In 1993, de Klerk and Mandela were awarded the Nobel Peace Prize for their efforts to bring reform and peace in South Africa. After the free elections of 1994, de Klerk was appointed the second vice president in President Mandela's cabinet. De Klerk and others resigned from their cabinet posts in 1996 to establish the **National Party** as an effective opposition party to the ANC. De Klerk retired from politics in 1997.

people joined in chorus to sing two national **anthems** and celebrate when the old flag and a new flag were raised. Over one billion people around the world watched the inauguration on television. It marked the true end of apartheid.

In his inauguration speech Mandela spoke of unity and "oneness". He said that he would work to build a place where people of all colours could live in peace, "a rainbow nation at peace with itself and the world". When he took power of the country, he did not look backwards to try to punish those who had **persecuted** him and other black and non-white people for so long. He praised those who had worked to end apartheid, and he spoke of working together to end all discrimination in South Africa for good. He wanted to ensure that South Africans would never again have to endure the pain of apartheid. He said: "The time for healing the wounds has come. The moment to bridge the **chasms** that divide us has come. The time to build is upon us."[2] Mandela's election was the first of many steps that the country would have to take towards healing its racial divisions. ❖

HEADLINES: 1918–1946

Here are some major news stories from the time of Nelson Mandela's childhood.

Allied victory! World War I over!

After four years, fourteen weeks, and two days, World War I came to an end on 11 November 1918, when Germany accepted the Allied armistice.

The conflict that led to World War I (1914–1918) began when Archduke Franz Ferdinand of Austria-Hungary was assassinated by a Bosnian man named Gavrilo Princip on 28 June 1914. Princip was a member of the Black Hand, a Serbian terrorist group that did not want the provinces of Bosnia and Herzegovina to be part of the Austro-Hungarian empire. Princip was charged with treason and murder, and was sentenced to 20 years in prison.

The assassination gave Austria-Hungary an excuse to take action against Serbia. As things escalated, other European powers were pulled into the conflict due to alliances that had previously been made. World War I was fought between 1914 and 1918 between the Allied (Entente) Powers and the Central Powers. The Allies were made up of the Russian Empire, France, the British Empire, Italy, the Empire of Japan, and the United States. The Central Powers consisted of Germany, Austria-Hungary, the Ottoman Empire, and Bulgaria.

Archduke Ferdinand can be seen here, moments before he was shot. It was his assassination that is seen as the spark that started World War I.

Revolution in Russia

In 1917, the **Bolsheviks** led a revolution in Russia, replacing the czars with a communist government. The revolution caused years of turmoil in Russia.

Lindbergh crosses Atlantic

In 1927, Charles Lindbergh became the first person to make a solo, non-stop flight across the Atlantic Ocean.

Wonder drug discovered?

Penicillin was first discovered by accident in 1928 by Sir Alexander Fleming. He had left his house for a month-long holiday. When he returned, he found mould growing in a dish. He noticed a difference around the edge of the bacteria from the rest of the bacteria. Fleming tried to reproduce it, but was unsuccessful. It took years and more scientists to finally find the drug that the world would come to rely on to fight infection. Many say it is the greatest discovery of all time.

Stock market crashes

In 1929, the U.S. stock market crashed, ushering in the Great Depression.

The Diary of a Young Girl published

When a Dutch Jewish girl named Anne Frank started to keep her diary, she could not have known that just a few weeks later she would be thrust into hiding from the Nazis. *The Diary of a Young Girl* was made up of excerpts from Anne Frank's real diary that she kept while hiding in the upper rooms of her house. She hid with her family for two years before being discovered in 1944. Anne Frank died in the Bergen-Belsen Nazi concentration camp. Her father, Otto, was the only family survivor of World War II (1939–1945) and keeper of Anne's diary.

Japan attacks Pearl Harbor!

On 7 December 1941, the Japanese launched a surprise attack on the U.S. naval base of Pearl Harbor in Hawaii. The result was that the U.S. entered World War II (1939–1945) on the side of the Allies.

Rolihlahla

Nelson Mandela was born on 18 July 1918, in Mvezo, a tiny village on the Mbashe River. Mvezo is located in the province of Transkei, which is now South Africa's Eastern Cape province. At his birth, however, Nelson was not his original name. Mandela's parents gave him the name Rolihlahla, which means "tree shaker". It was later, in a British school, that he would be given the name of Nelson. Mandela's people also used the name Rolihlahla to mean "troublemaker". Perhaps his destiny was laid out at this point. Nelson Rolihlahla Mandela would definitely shake things up in his world.

MANDELA'S FAMILY

Mandela's father was named Gadla Hendry Mphakanyiswa, known as Hendry. He was a man of royal blood of an important people of South Africa called the Thembu tribe. He was tall and proud, but also stubborn. He had 4 wives and 13 children. Mandela's mother, Nosekeni Fanny, was his third wife. Hendry was the headman of Mvezo. He performed ceremonies such as marriages and funerals. He was also employed by the British authorities to make sure the local villagers paid their taxes.

Hendry's stubbornness got him into trouble a year after Mandela was born. He became involved in a fight with a local white government official. Because Hendry refused to give in, he lost his job and most of his possessions. He was no longer able to support his very large family. Hendry relocated the young Rolihlahla and his mother to the village of Qunu. Nosekeni had relatives there who could help.

MANDELA THE BOY

Mandela would spend his next few years in Qunu. Despite the fact that his family had fallen on hard times, Mandela would look back fondly on this period of his life. The humble home consisted of three round huts fenced off with poles. These huts had been crafted out of mud bricks by Mandela's mother. One hut was used for sleeping, one for cooking, and one for storing food. The roof was made of bundles of dried grass tied together with rope. Chairs and cupboards were made of earth, and the family slept on mats. Nelson and his mother lived in these huts with his two sisters, Mabel and Leabie. They shared food and happy times with an extended family of uncles, aunts, cousins, and friends.[4]

When Mandela was five years old, he started helping the other country boys herd the village sheep and cattle from pasture to pasture. The boys also had fun entertaining themselves in the countryside of Qunu. Mandela kept this attachment to Qunu as he grew older, remembering it fondly even while in prison. Eventually he would return to the hills and streams of his boyhood home, when he retired in 1999.

> "It was there in the hills and valleys of Qunu; in the rolling hills of KwaDlangezwa; in the Genadendal settlement; and along the Gariep, the Lekoa, and the Luvuvhu Rivers that we first understood that we are not free. It is there that we were inspired with pride in our history. There, among the humble but proud rural folk, we learnt of the courage of our forebears in the face of superior force."[5]

> – Speech made by Mandela at the Freedom Day Celebrations, Umtata, 27 April 1999

At this time, when Mandela was a young boy, some black people of the Transkei region, including Mandela's father, Hendry, still practised traditional beliefs. This included a belief in God, the supreme creator. However, the Xhosa people see God as far off and not affecting their

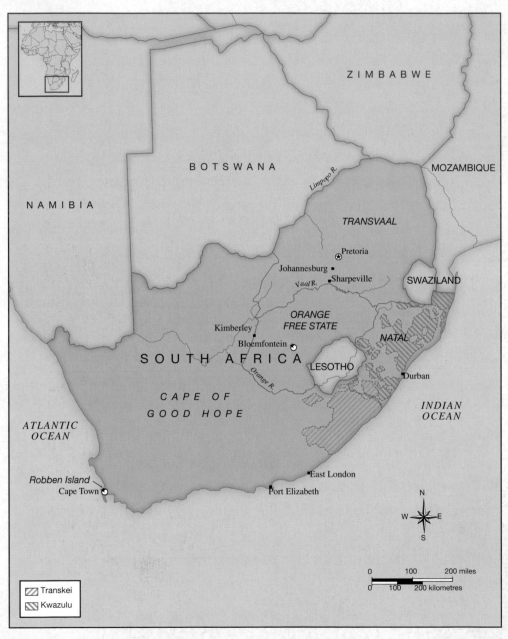

This map shows a broad overview of South Africa and neighbouring countries as of 1994. Please refer back to this page throughout the book.

South African colonial history

In order to understand the world in which Mandela grew up in South Africa, it is helpful to know a little about the history of the region. In the past few hundred years, it is one of **colonial** incursion from Europe, with most of those years representing forced white dominance and control. This is the world Hendry knew and Mandela fought to overcome.

Battles for land in South Africa date back hundreds of years. The Dutch first landed in South Africa in the late 1500s. They did not intend to build a colony in South Africa, but they started farming and growing their businesses. Soon the population grew. For many years the Dutch people and the native inhabitants of Africa lived in peace. But when the Dutch decided to make permanent settlements, conflict between the Dutch and the Khoikhoi, a race of people native to South Africa, began.

The Dutch had assigned land rights to many farmers. They felt that land could be owned, but the Khoikhoi were a nomadic people. They believed that they should be free to go anywhere and to let their animals graze on any land. It had been that way for centuries in Africa, and the Khoikhoi felt it should stay that way. They fought to regain their rights to the land, but lost. The Dutch continued to control much of the land in South Africa and colonized more, moving north. Many wars were fought between the Dutch and native African people over the right to live on and move across the land.

The Dutch had originally agreed not to enslave native people. However, in the 1700s, with the Dutch population growing, they began to do just that. The native people fought back, fighting not only for their land, but for their freedom. Dutch rule eventually prevailed, however.

In the 1800s, rule of the Cape in South Africa moved from the Dutch to the British, causing even more conflict in the region. The Dutch, the British, and the native African people were all fighting for the same land. War broke out between the Dutch farmers, called Boers, and the British. After almost three years of war, called the Boer Wars or Anglo-Boer Wars, the Dutch and British eventually decided to join forces. They formed the Union of South Africa. With this union, they secured white rule. Then they passed laws that discriminated against black people and other non-white Africans. Among other things, these laws limited where black people could travel, what work they could do, and what land they could own. The best jobs were given to white people, and the 1913 Land Act saved 90 per cent of the land for only whites to own.

lives very much. They believe ancestral spirits are closer to us, and affect our daily lives all the time. It is important to make sacrifices to these ancestral spirits in order to keep them happy. The spirits will then watch over the home and family. This is what Hendry believed. Others in the Transkei had converted to Christianity. Mandela's family had close Christian friends. Eventually, Mandela's mother converted to **Methodism** and had Rolihlahla **baptized**. She and Hendry then decided to send Mandela to the local Christian **mission** school. Mandela would be the first family member to attend that school. Many children educated in mission schools were named after British heroes. At the age of seven, Rolihlahla was given a new first name. His teacher told him his new name would be Nelson.[6]

EDUCATION IN LEADERSHIP

In 1927, when Mandela was nine, his father died after suffering from lung disease. Hendry's friend Jongintaba, the **regent** of the Tembu people and head of the Madiba clan, agreed to adopt Mandela. Mandela's mother took him on a daylong journey, by foot, from Qunu to Mqhekezweni (another Transkei village), where the regent presided, or exercised control, over his people. Mqhekezweni was known as the "Great Place". A visitor might think Mqhekezweni to be small and remote by today's Western standards. However, the young Mandela would have been impressed, and it would have seemed like a city compared to what he was used to in Qunu. The nine-year-old Mandela

"One of the marks of a great chief is the ability to keep together all sections of his people."
—Nelson Mandela

What's in a name?

Nelson Rolihlahla Mandela has gone by several names in his life. Eventually he made it known that he preferred his clan name, "Madiba". Here are some of Mandela's names:

Rolihlahla	birth name; means "tree shaker" or "troublemaker"
Nelson	British name given to him by his teacher at mission school
Madiba	name of the clan of which Mandela is a member; also the name of a Thembu chief who ruled in the Transkei in the 18th century
Tata	Xhosa word meaning "father", often used by South Africans to describe Mandela, since they see him as a father figure
Khulu	means "Great One"; also a shortened version of the Xhosa word "uBawomkhulu", which means "grandfather"
Dalibhunga	name given to Mandela after the traditional Xhosa rite of passage into manhood; it means "creator of the council", or "convener of the dialogue"

arrived wearing an old shirt, shorts cut from a pair of his father's old trousers, and a piece of string for a belt.[7]

It was in Mqhekezweni that Mandela saw what it was like to be a respected leader. He watched how Jongintaba ruled, and how his people welcomed him. These years would influence Mandela in his own life and ambitions. Mandela was serious and worked hard. He did well in the mission school, and he began to learn English. Already, people could see he had leadership qualities. Mandela also made a new friend in Justice, the regent's son and **heir**. Justice was four years older, handsome, athletic, and popular. Mandela quickly came to **idolize** him.[8]

When Nelson was not at school or studying, he also had chores. One of his chores was to iron the chief's suits. Nelson took particular pride in

Nelson Mandela in his youth.

this job, carefully ironing the creases in the suit trousers.[9] Mandela would always have an interest in clothing and a reputation for dressing well and looking good as he grew up.

Another part of Mandela's education was watching how Jongintaba ruled as regent. Mandela loved to watch tribal meetings. Here, the regent would listen patiently all day as tribesmen, who had travelled miles, complained to him and sought his advice. The regent would then come to a decision, trying to take in all of the opinions and complaints. While in prison, Mandela would write about these memories:

> "One of the marks of a great chief is the ability to keep together all sections of his people… and on major questions there are sometimes sharp differences of opinion. The Mqhekezweni court was particularly strong, and the regent was able to carry the whole community because the court was representative of all shades of opinion."[10]

During this time Mandela would also learn about his **ancestors**. Visiting tribal chiefs were excellent storytellers, and they told Mandela of the great heroes and history of his people. They spoke of a time before the white **colonial** rulers came, when they were the masters of their own land. This was also the first Mandela heard about the prison on Robben Island, where some of his heroes had been sent by the British. He could not have guessed that he, too, would one day be jailed there.

"He was seen as a young man who knew how to express his views."
—Chief Anderson Joyi,
recalling Mandela as a boy

BECOMING A MAN

> "He was seen as a young man who knew how to express his views. And the people of the Thembus were very proud of that when they saw him even at that time as a leader."[11]

—Chief Anderson Joyi, recalling Mandela as a boy.

At age 16 Mandela went through the Xhosa rite of manhood, which is a ritual completing the journey of a boy becoming a man. In this tradition, boys first go through circumcision, where the foreskin is cut from the penis. After this painful procedure, they live in isolation while healing. They smear white clay on their bodies during this time and bury their foreskin as a symbol of putting their childhood behind them. Being of royal blood, Mandela would be expected to hold office in his life. No Xhosa from a rural area could take office without having gone through this ritual. The regent and elders would watch to make sure the boys had courage during their circumcisions. Mandela later admitted that the pain was horrible, and that he was not as strong as the other boys. However, he was able to yell "I am a man!" after his circumcision, which is what he was expected to do.[12]

Mandela was then sent to boarding school at the Methodist institution of Clarkebury, where the regent and his son, Justice, had been educated. By this time, in 1934, Clarkebury was the largest educational centre in Transkei (now an area of Eastern Cape province). The school was run by the Reverend Cecil Harris, who was very strict. Mandela met many lifelong friends at Clarkebury. He was exposed to many different people from many different places, both men and women at the **co-educational** school. Apartheid had not yet come to South Africa at this time.

HEALDTOWN

After two years at Clarkebury, Mandela was sent to a larger Methodist school called Healdtown. He was again following the same path the regent's son, Justice, had taken. Healdtown, like Clarkebury, was run by the Methodist British. Despite the Christian influence in his education, Mandela never became a true believer. He did adapt to the strict atmosphere, however, and carried the discipline and mental training with him throughout his life. Mandela always rose early, and he disapproved of heavy drinking and swearing. While Mandela was being educated in British-run schools, he still remembered his roots and took great pride in his Xhosa culture. In 1938, Mandela was delighted when a noted Xhosa poet named Krune Mqhayi visited his college carrying spears and dressed in traditional Xhosa fashion to perform a Xhosa essay Nelson had written.[13]

Mandela also took an interest in boxing and running at Healdtown. He preferred these individual sports to team sports. Mandela was not a brilliant student, but he had a good memory and worked hard. He took his studies seriously, but his heroes were mostly athletes at this time. He became close friends with several Xhosa boys who would later join him in the **African National Congress (ANC)**. He also made friends outside

African National Congress (ANC)

The African National Congress formed in 1912 in response to the creation of the Union of South Africa, which solidified white minority rule. The ANC was the first African liberation movement. From the beginning, it represented a variety of people and groups. The goal of the ANC was to bring all Africans together as one people to defend their rights and freedoms.

However, the ANC had little influence until the 1940s, when Mandela and other young activists gained support for protests against the apartheid government. Once apartheid was ending in the early 1990s, the ANC emerged as the primary political party, with the most support around the nation.

of his tribe, including his **Sotho**-speaking housemaster, the Reverend Seth Mokitimi. Mokitimi pushed through changes at Healdtown to give students better food and more freedom. He later became the first black president of the Methodist Church.

In 1936, there were protests in South Africa when the government took away more rights of blacks. However, Mandela was not very aware of politics at this time. Even though the ANC had been set up in 1912, Mandela first heard about it while at Healdtown. The mission teachers at Healdtown assumed political protestors were "agitators", or "troublemakers". Mandela was not yet a troublemaker. He was still not sure what to make of the two sides of British influence on his homeland. On the one hand, his people, the Xhosa, had been defeated and subjugated (brought under control) by the British. On the other hand, he realized the opportunity for wealth and success that his **liberal** British education could provide.

In 1938, at age 20, Mandela graduated from Healdtown. The next year he would attend the university at Fort Hare, a few miles away. He would also leave behind his friends for the first time, including Justice, who would remain at Healdtown.

COLLEGE AT FORT HARE

The tiny South African Native College at Fort Hare was the only black university in South Africa. When Mandela arrived, there were fewer than 200 students. The school was supported by the surrounding universities and made up of some of the brightest black South Africans. The university at Fort Hare was a famous college, and Mandela was glad to be there. His adopted father, the regent, was glad to have a member of his clan attending. The teachers at Fort Hare thought of their students as the future leaders of their people.

Mandela found a new friend at Fort Hare in his nephew Kaiser Matanzima. Matanzima was also from the royal Tembu family. Even

South Africa and World War II

The white community of South Africa was divided in its loyalties when World War II broke out in 1939. Some wanted to remain neutral. There were also supporters of both Britain and Germany, on opposite sides in the war. At this time South Africa was part of the Commonwealth of Nations, or simply **Commonwealth**. This is a voluntary association of independent states, most of which were formerly part of the British Empire. Members of the Commonwealth agree to certain values and goals – free trade, the rule of law, individual liberty, etc. – and cooperate to promote them around the world.

Eventually, the pro-British side prevailed, and South Africa sent troops to fight on the British side in North Africa and Europe. However, pro-German, anti-war elements of South Africa remained, and many would later come to be the architects and supporters of apartheid.

though he was Mandela's nephew, Matanzima was older and more confident. Matanzima encouraged Mandela, and they spent a lot of time together. Even though they would later become political rivals, both Mandela and Matanzima valued this friendship.

Mandela excelled at Fort Hare. He did well at cross-country running and boxing. He also liked ballroom dancing and acting. Some of Mandela's friends were active in politics. Mandela's only ambition at the time, however, was to be a court interpreter. South Africa has many languages, and the court interpreter acts as a neutral party in court, assisting communication between the prosecution and defence. This was a respected position in the rural areas of South Africa. Mandela studied interpreting, as well as law, native administration, English, and politics. When Great Britain declared war on Germany in 1939, and South Africa entered the war on Britain's side, Mandela supported the fight against Hitler.

STUBBORN SPIRIT

In his second year at Fort Hare, Mandela was elected to the Students' Representative Council. However, only one quarter of the students voted. The majority of students **boycotted** the election, demanding better college food and greater powers for the council. Mandela and the other five representatives resigned. The principal ordered new elections, but again the majority of students refused to vote, and again the same six students were elected. Mandela felt he must consider the views of the majority, and so he resigned again, even though the other five elected students chose to stay on the council.

Mandela was warned that he would be expelled if he did not serve on the council. But that didn't scare him. He refused to return to the council, and was expelled from Fort Hare. He went home to the regent, who was angry. He felt the young Mandela was throwing away his career. And then, the regent gave Mandela news that would shake up his life again. He had arranged for Mandela to be married and settle down with his own family. He had made similar arrangements for his son Justice. This was a breaking point for Mandela. He did not want to marry the arranged girl, and he knew she didn't want to marry him. At age 22, Mandela decided to run away with Justice to Johannesburg, the largest city and cultural centre of South Africa.

JOHANNESBURG

Mandela and Justice came to Johannesburg in 1941, at a time when many blacks were arriving in the city looking for work. The demand for war-related materials during World War II (1939–1945) helped industry in the cities, and there were jobs to be had. **Afrikaner** whites who were already established in Johannesburg felt threatened by the new competition. They began to call for more extreme forms of **segregation**. They called this *apartheid*, which meant "apartness". Mandela and Justice took jobs at one of the mining companies, where there was strict segregation of blacks and whites. Black workers made up most of the labour force, and they were cut off from the rest of the city in enclosed compounds. They also made less money, with chiefs in rural areas helping to provide the mines with cheap labour. Mandela worked as a night watchman.

When Mandela boasted that he had run away from home and the regent, he was fired from his job and told to return home. He quickly learned that, despite his royal heritage, he was a nobody in Johannesburg. Mandela was desperate for a job, so his cousin sent him to see Walter Sisulu, a black estate agent in Johannesburg. Mandela and Sisulu recognized great things in each other. At this difficult time in his life, Mandela found a **mentor** and partner in Sisulu.

Townships

Under apartheid, townships were urban living areas reserved by the government for non-whites. They were usually built on the edges of towns and cities. The apartheid government of South Africa forced blacks to move from areas designated as "white-only" into these townships, which were often underdeveloped with poorer living conditions.

A TASTE OF LAW AND POLITICS

Mandela had ideas of becoming a lawyer. Sisulu managed to get him a job as a law clerk. Mandela lived in a black slum in Alexandra at this point, which was a township 9.5 kilometres (6 miles) north of the city with no electricity. Mandela was very poor, and sometimes had to walk 19 kilometres (12 miles) a day to and from the office in order to save money. But, he was finally able to fend for himself in the city by late 1941. He was also brought into politics for the first time by Walter Sisulu, who had joined the ANC in 1940. The frustrations and humiliations he experienced as a black man in the white man's city also influenced Mandela and made him take a greater interest in politics. When an office friend of his, Gaur Radebe, organized a bus boycott after the fares were raised, Mandela joined the boycott and marched with 10,000 other blacks. The buses were empty for nine days, and the fare was changed back to its lower rate. It was a taste of political success and power.

Mandela soon moved to Orlando, a planned township suburb 19 kilometres (12 miles) outside Johannesburg. It didn't feel as comfortable to Mandela in some ways, but he now lived close to his friend Sisulu.[14]

MEETING EVELYN

In Orlando at this time, Mandela was always well dressed. He was popular with many women. In 1944, Walter Sisulu married a woman named Albertina. Mandela spent a lot of time at their house. When Walter's young cousin Evelyn Mase arrived from the Transkei to become a nurse, Nelson was quickly attracted to her. Soon they were going out together, and within months they were married. A year later, Evelyn gave birth to their son, Thembi. The couple would have four children, though one died in infancy. Although Evelyn was not interested in politics, she encouraged her husband, at first.

YOUTH LEAGUE AND POLITICS

Sisulu was involved with the ANC, which was growing. By age 25, Mandela was also committed to the ANC and its politics. At the same time, Mandela was studying for a law degree. However, he was beginning to see his future in politics. Mandela and a group of young blacks, including Sisulu and another friend Oliver Tambo, now wanted to form a Youth League within the ANC. Having seen the success of the bus boycott, they wanted to use this group to organize similar protests. In April of 1944, the Youth League was officially launched. It was open to anyone between the ages of 12 and 40. The goal of the ANC Youth League was to breathe new life into the ANC and transform it into a party of mass protest.

The **Allies** won the war in 1945, which represented a triumph over **fascism**. But a victory for the Soviet Union, which was one of the Allies, also represented a victory for **communism**. In South Africa after the war, communism and nationalism competed for the support of smart young leaders like Mandela. Mandela was a nationalist, but he noticed that the communists welcomed all the races and treated them equally. The nationalism he was a part of was not interested in welcoming non-black Africans. Also, the ANC made its dislike of the communists loud and clear. For the time being, Mandela shared that dislike and thought that black Africans would do best for themselves on their own, as would the other oppressed races of South Africa.

PROTEST AND CRACKDOWN

In 1946, the recently formed African Mineworkers' Union led a strike of 70,000 black miners. With the support of the white **United Party** government of Jan Smuts, the mining companies forced workers back down into the mines. Hundreds were wounded and nine were killed. Days later, many of the leaders were fined or imprisoned. Mandela knew some of the strikers, and he was moved by their bravery and how they stuck together. Again he saw the potential to bring about change through mass protest, when people were able to work as a team. ❖

HEADLINES: 1947–1961

Here are some major news stories from Mandela's early years of fighting apartheid.

India gains independence

In 1947, India gained its independence after more than 200 years of British rule.

King George VI dead at 56

The United Kingdom's King George VI died in 1952 and was replaced by his daughter, who became Queen Elizabeth II at the age of 25.

Rock and Roll sweeps the world!

Alan Freed, a disc jockey in Cleveland, Ohio, in the United States, first used the term "rock and roll" in 1951. The music took off. The record that many consider to be the first rock and roll record, Ike Turner's *Rocket 88*, was released that year. The music genre gained the immediate and frenzied support of the teen population. Soon, the music became a regular and important part of UK and U.S. society.

Hemingway awarded Nobel Prize

In 1954, Ernest Hemingway (1899–1961) was awarded the Nobel Prize for Literature. Hemingway got his start in writing as a newspaper reporter. His writing was influenced by his experiences in Europe during World War I (1914–1918) and the Spanish Civil War (1936–1939), as well as his interest in sports, such as fishing, hunting, and bullfighting. His most famous works include: *The Sun Also Rises*, *A Farewell to Arms*, *For Whom the Bell Tolls*, and *The Old Man and the Sea*.

East Germans build wall separating East from West

Following World War II (1939–1945), control of Germany and the city of Berlin were divided among the victorious powers. Great Britain and the United States combined their parts, which formed a democratic West Germany. However, the Soviet Union decided to maintain control of its portion. East Germany became a communist, Soviet-controlled state.

Soldiers work to build the Berlin Wall in 1961.

In 1961, in order to keep people from escaping to the West, East Germany built a wall dividing the two parts of the country. Half of the city of Berlin was in West Germany, and half was in East Germany. The Berlin Wall divided the city and the country, and it was a symbol of the Cold War for 28 years. Over 100 people died over the years trying to cross the wall into West Berlin. East Germany finally opened its borders in 1989, and the wall was dismantled. Germany was officially reunified the following year, in 1990.

Speaking out

*The government's crushing of the mine **strike** was a sign of things to come. Mandela would again be shocked at the government's next crackdown. There were over 300,000 Indians living in South Africa by this time, and history had given them their own experience of discrimination and protest in the country. In 1946, the government introduced the Asiatic Land Tenure Bill, also known as the "Indian Ghetto Act". This banned the sale of any more land to Indians. The Indians again relied on organized, **passive resistance**. Two thousand protestors went to jail. It was another example of solidarity in peaceful protest. The ANC now decided to ally itself with the Indian political groups in South Africa.*

In 1947, India won its independence from Great Britain. This was an inspirational example of successful resistance to power. Mandela admired people like Gandhi in India, as well as the Indian protestors of South Africa. However, at this time, he still thought the races could best fight for their rights on their own. Of course, he had no idea how long the fight would take, and he was optimistic at this point. He knew for certain that apartheid could not last in the long run; it was on the wrong side of history. He felt that the tide might be turning against the National Party.

He would soon find out how wrong he was, and how hard the white leaders would fight to maintain their control.

ENTER APARTHEID

In 1948, the **National Party** surprisingly gained votes and was elected on a platform of apartheid, or "apartness". The National Party was mostly made up of Afrikaner nationalists (whites of Dutch descent) who had not supported working with the United Party, nor helping the British in World War II. The election of the National Party marked a turning point for South Africa. Apartheid meant a movement toward a complete separation of the races in South Africa, by force of law. Mandela, along with many of his ANC friends, was stunned.[1]

The Prohibition of Mixed Marriages Act of 1949 meant that people of different races could no longer marry. Families could also be broken up if the husband and wife ended up with different race classifications. The Population Registration Act of 1950 required that every person be

Black labourers at the Sallies Mine, near Johannesburg, South Africa, 1948. These men are working to extract gold from solid rock. In this physically demanding job, only one quarter of a gram of gold could be extracted from five tonnes of gold-bearing rock.

Verwoerd's twisted vision

Once elected under the platform of apartheid in 1948, the National Party held control in South Africa for almost 46 years. Hendrik Frensch Verwoerd (fur-VOORT) was the man behind the idea of apartheid. He had admired and studied the Nazis of Germany, and the apartheid system and policies he proposed showed their racially-oppressive influence. In 1950, Verwoerd became South Africa's minister of native affairs and put his apartheid ideas into practice, working towards the goal of complete racial separation. Things would get worse before they got better – Verwoerd became prime minister in 1958.

classified by race. After this, every aspect of life in South Africa would depend upon a person's racial classification. The Reservation of Separate Amenities Act of 1953 allowed the government to offer not only segregated, but inferior facilities to non-whites. The races were completely separated in schools, hospitals, sports, and living areas. It is estimated that apartheid laws forced 3.5 million people from their homes.[2]

In the face of these extreme measures, protests arose. The government only responded more harshly. The Suppression of Communism Act of 1950 gave the government the power to banish anyone seeking social or political changes or creating disorder by encouraging angry feelings between whites and non-whites. At the time, Mandela still argued for black-only protests, but his ANC friends insisted they should include all anti-apartheid groups. Mandela's views began to change. Sisulu asked Mandela to organize the ANC office in Johannesburg leading up to a strike in 1950 in protest of the Suppression of Communism Act. This was an important job that made him a key figure in a major national protest. It also put him in a position where he worked alongside activists of other races. Mandela was becoming a practical politician, and he realized the ANC needed help. It didn't matter if the help came from Indians or whites, African nationalists or communists. Though he was still known only locally and in the struggle, Mandela's political skills and wider vision would propel him to further influence in the coming years.[3]

THE DEFIANCE CAMPAIGN

In 1952, the ANC demanded that the government repeal (scrap) major apartheid laws, and it promised a national campaign of non-violent resistance to oppose apartheid and the government if its demands were not met. The non-violent Defiance Campaign would be modelled on the example of Mohandas Gandhi. It was a program of civil disobedience, or passive resistance, that would purposely defy the government's racial laws and welcome imprisonment. Mandela joined a committee of four that drafted a letter to Prime Minister Dr Malan demanding the repeal of the most unjust laws.

Mandela had been elected president of the ANC Youth League in 1950. Now, with his direct role in the defiance against apartheid, he was looking more and more like a leader. Mandela offered to take the key position of the campaign, responsible for national recruitment, a mission that would have him travelling across the country. He became more well known. The date of 26 June 1952 was set for the beginning of the

Passbooks

After the Population Registration Act of 1950, everyone classified as "black" was required by the government to carry a passbook, which contained fingerprints, a photo, and information on what access the person had to non-black areas. This was part of the apartheid system to enforce complete separation of the races. It allowed the white government to regulate where black people could live and even visit in South Africa.

resistance campaign. Four days before that, Mandela spoke to 10,000 people, the largest audience he had ever addressed. He spoke to them about the history they were making with their united resistance. Mandela received long applause and found the experience exciting.[4]

On the night of the first day of resistance, 26 June, Mandela went to jail for the first time. He and fellow protestors were rounded up by police that night for violating an 11p.m. curfew. He spent two nights in a crowded jail before being released. The conditions were horrible, and Mandela would remember the police brutality. The peaceful resistance called the Defiance Campaign continued, and Mandela was its main organizer. People all over the country peacefully protested over the next months. Over 8,000 people went to jail for things such as marching into whites-only areas and violating curfews. Mandela travelled across the country, often from house to house, explaining the cause of the resistance campaign and recruiting new activists. The harsh reaction of the South African government in sending so many peaceful protestors to jail had an interesting effect. Among the non-white people of South Africa, the Defiance Campaign made going to jail seem like a distinction of self-sacrifice for a greater cause.

GOVERNMENT RESPONSE

The police cracked down with raids. In July of 1952, Mandela was arrested on the charge of violating the Suppression of Communism Act of 1950. Twenty other leaders of the Defiance Campaign around the country were also arrested. One of the organizers decided to look after his own interests, and he named his friends as communists. It was not surprising to anyone that they were found guilty. The judge in this case, however, passed down a fairly light sentence. The sentence was nine months of imprisonment with hard labour, but was suspended for two years. In October of 1952, Mandela was easily elected as the president of the **Transvaal** ANC (a regional branch of the ANC). This made him very popular with the protestors. It also made him a target for the government.

His first prison experience

Mandela would never forget his first experience of being locked up at the beginning of the Defiance Campaign in June of 1952, when he spent two nights in jail. The conditions were horrible. Mandela recalled later how one of the prisoners was pushed down the stairs by the police, and was then left to spend the night untreated, in extreme pain.[5]

The previous president of the ANC in South Africa had been banned from holding a position in the ANC and from attending meetings. This was one of the government's weapons in its push to destroy the Defiance Campaign. Despite his popular election, Mandela's presidency of the Transvaal ANC didn't last long. In December of 1952, like his predecessor, the government banned Mandela for six months from attending any meetings and even from talking to more than one person at a time. He was also forbidden to leave Johannesburg without government permission. While this technically made his position as president illegal, it also had the effect of boosting Mandela's reputation as an active leader, willing to sacrifice for the cause.

As the resistance campaign continued, the government's harsh response to peaceful protest had an effect that was opposite to what they intended. The ANC, as a seeming victim of government suppression, had become a popular movement. The government was not finished, however, and became even more determined to crack down.

By the end of 1952, the government had passed the Public Safety Act and the Criminal Laws Amendment Act. These acts made the purposeful breaking of the law punishable by up to three years in jail and whipping. Mandela and his friends were surprised at the harshness of the penalties. By the end of that year, the Defiance Campaign was over. It had not had much effect on the whites of South Africa, nor on public opinion outside of the country. However, it had helped dramatically increase membership in the ANC, and it had given Mandela a boost of self-confidence as the campaign's organizer. His experiences had also changed his mind. Mandela now realized that the fight against apartheid would be a greater cause, with more support, if it welcomed people of all races.[6]

In the meantime, in 1952, Mandela partnered with Oliver Tambo to start the first black African law firm in South Africa. The two had been friends since attending Fort Hare together, and were both part of the ANC Youth League. Their law offices were in the same building as the ANC headquarters, and they became the official attorneys for the ANC. Mandela and Tambo law offices represented other black clients, and many rural people who were being kicked off their land by the government. Tambo later remembered the long queues of people overflowing into the corridors, and how every visit to a jailed client reminded them of the suffering of their people at the hands of the National Party government.[7]

A TURN TOWARDS ARMED RESISTANCE

Mandela's frustration grew as the government cracked down even harder and refused to budge. Mandela did not believe that passive resistance alone was necessarily the answer for the ANC. He admired Gandhi and his methods, but Mandela was interested in whatever methods would get results.

The government's banning of ANC leaders marked a turning point. In 1953, Mandela argued that the ANC should change its strategy from one of peaceful resistance to one of armed, militant resistance. His friends and colleagues rejected the idea of turning to violence. Nonetheless, Mandela secretly arranged for his friend Sisulu to go to China to try to get weapons for the cause. The Chinese wanted nothing to do with it, and wisely cautioned against an armed struggle. Sisulu agreed with that advice, and Mandela realized later in life that he had been too hotheaded at this point in the struggle.[8]

CONGRESS OF THE PEOPLE

In 1953, Z. K. Matthews, one of Mandela's mentors at Fort Hare, formally proposed a national convention, or Congress of the People. This Congress of the People would represent all the people of South Africa, regardless of race or colour. The purpose of the Congress of the People would be to create a Freedom Charter for South Africa's future. Mandela, whose government ban expired in June that year, welcomed the idea, and thought the historic meeting would be of great importance. He had a hand in the final edit of the charter.[9]

The Congress of the People met on 26 June 1955. Three thousand representatives came from all over the country. Mandela was still banned by the government from attending meetings, but he watched it from a distance. On the first day, the Freedom Charter was read in three languages and approved with enthusiastic shouts from the crowd. The second day, as sections of the Charter were being read, police burst into the crowd. They announced that they were investigating for high treason (acts or attempts to overthrow the government), and took down every name before allowing people to leave.

"…they defended our people who were in difficulties ... Africans were carrying passes, and they were arrested at every little excuse, by the police."
—Adelaide Tambo, speaking about
the Mandela & Tambo Law firm

MANDELA & TAMBO LAW OFFICES

When Mandela wasn't working for the ANC, he was pursuing his law practice with his friend and partner Tambo. Mandela was gaining a reputation as a leader and a fearless lawyer. The Mandela and Tambo law firm became the official representation for the ANC. They were also in demand from other black clients, some of whom had simply been arrested for not having their passes. Peasants from rural areas came to complain about the government kicking them off land that had been in their families for generations.

> "They were a practice that was politically linked, because they defended our people who were in difficulties. Of course, like all lawyers they charged fees, but no one was turned away at Mandela & Tambo, because they did not have money. Those were the days of pettiness [small-mindedness] of the regime. Africans were carrying passes, and they were arrested at every little excuse, by the police. The office was always full of people who came there to ask for help. But, of course, they dealt with many other cases, civil cases, and people came with other problems. Divorce cases, violence, where people were stabbed or people were shot dead. Things like that. A lot of cases went there."[10]
>
> – Adelaide Tambo, wife of Oliver Tambo

EXIT EVELYN

During these political events of the early 1950s, Mandela's home life was becoming strained. Evelyn was becoming increasingly religious, and she now hated Mandela's political involvement, which went against her beliefs as a Jehovah's Witness. (Jehovah's Witnesses try to bring others into their faith, in which they believe in the rule of God, the sinfulness of organized religions and governments, and a certain and approaching millennium, or period of one thousand years, when Christ will rule on a holy Earth.) Between politics and law, Mandela was hardly ever at home with Evelyn and the children. Eventually, Evelyn gave Mandela a choice between her and the family on one hand, and his political involvements on the other. This was a choice Mandela could not make, as he was also "married" to the ANC cause. Unable to work out their differences, Evelyn left Mandela in December of 1955 and took the children. She brought up the children on her own. Later in life Mandela would acknowledge that he was too distant as a father, and his children grew up without his help.[11]

TREASON TRIAL

In 1956, the ANC organized a conference in order to adopt the Freedom Charter. The Freedom Charter, a call for equal status for people of all races, was eventually approved by the conference. The effect was that Mandela was arrested the morning of 5 December 1956, on a charge of high treason. Another 155 leaders from the Congress of the People were also arrested on the same charge over the next ten days. The penalty for high treason, if convicted, would be death.

The Freedom Charter

The Freedom Charter included a demand for a democratically elected, multi-racial government, and equal opportunities for all. It also called for the nationalization of banks and heavy industries, as well as a redistribution of land. It opens with the following:

"We, the people of South Africa, declare for all our country and the world to know:

That South Africa belongs to all who live in it, black and white, and that no government can justly claim authority unless it is based on the will of the people."[12]

Involvement with the Congress of the People and the Freedom Charter were the main basis for the government's charge of high treason. The **prosecution** argued that the accused men were involved in a countrywide **conspiracy** to use violence to overthrow the government and replace it with a communist state. At first, Mandela didn't take it all that seriously, despite the attempts of police to humiliate prisoners. However, he soon realized that the trial would be much longer than he originally thought.

The preliminary hearings began in January 1957. These were simply to determine if there was enough of a case for the trial to go before the Supreme Court. They dragged on for months. The government continued to bring in bumbling witnesses and false evidence. The trial as a whole would stretch on for more than four years. Mandela did manage a brighter spot in his life during this time. Not long after his divorce from Evelyn in 1957, Mandela met a social worker named Nomzamo Winifred Madikizela, known as Winnie. He was immediately taken by this beautiful younger woman. Mandela announced on their first date that he would marry her. While the treason trial was still going on, in 1958, Mandela and Winnie were married. It was about a year after that first date.[13]

While the treason trial was going on, Dr Hendrik Verwoerd became prime minister of South Africa in 1958. Mandela knew that the new

The trial

During the trial, Mandela mounted an eloquent defence. When asked whether the Defiance Campaign of 1952 had any results, Mandela replied:

"Yes, most certainly. Firstly, it pricked the conscience of the European public which became aware in a much more clear manner of the sufferings and disabilities of the African people…. It also led to discussions on the policies of apartheid at the United Nations and I think to that extent it was an outstanding success."[14]

Nelson and Winnie Mandela.

government, run by the architect of apartheid, would be ruthless. In 1959, a black-nationalist group called the Pan-Africanist Congress (PAC) was formed. In 1960, the PAC announced a day of protest in black townships. The ANC was preparing for a mass demonstration against passbook laws on 31 March 1960. The PAC decided to push ahead with its own anti-pass campaign before the ANC's. The problem was that the PAC's campaign had much less planning.

SHARPEVILLE MASSACRE

The PAC's idea was for men to leave their passbooks at home and surrender themselves for arrest at police stations around the country. In Cape Town 1,500 people offered themselves for arrest and huge crowds gathered. Two people were killed by police. Things were worse in Sharpeville, where a crowd of about 10,000 surrounded the police station. The police opened fire and killed over 60 people. Many more were wounded. The government immediately took the opportunity to declare a state of emergency and proceeded to hold over 2,000 people.

News of the Sharpeville massacre spread around the world. There was international protest, and the United Nations (UN) condemned the attack and called upon the South African government to end apartheid. Mandela thought the tide had turned, but he again underestimated how far the government would go to protect its authority. On 8 April 1960, the government pushed through an Unlawful Organizations Bill that finally made the ANC illegal. It would remain an illegal organization, working underground, for the next 30 years.

Finally, in March of 1961, after over four years of the treason trial, the judge ruled there was no proof that the accused wanted violent revolution. Mandela and his colleagues were **acquitted**. With the ANC now an illegal organization, however, he and his friends agreed that Mandela should now take his fight underground.

ANC and PAC

The PAC was founded in 1959 by dissatisfied black members of the ANC who felt that working with Indians, "coloureds" (those of mixed race), and whites would not help black people gain political control of South Africa. Because of its black nationalist stance, the PAC was a rival of the ANC, and the two organizations fought for support among black South Africans, even though they occasionally cooperated for similar goals. The government tried to pit such rival activist organizations against each other to prevent minority groups from uniting to form a majority with even more support.

HIDING OUT

Mandela would become more famous in hiding than ever before, and he was soon seen as the chief spokesman for his people. Various supporters set up **safe houses** and helped Mandela hide and move around in secret. At one point, Mandela's white journalist friend Wolfie Kodesh hid him in a one-room apartment in a white suburb of Johannesburg. Because of racial attitudes, it was thought the police would never suspect that Mandela would be hiding there. From hiding, Mandela continued to argue for non-violent protest. Mandela was able to thrill the audience at the All-In African Conference with a dramatic speech in 1961. He also began organizing a massive strike that would take place on 31 May.

With the PAC working against the strike, and the press publicizing warnings against it beforehand, the protest was not the success Mandela had hoped. Mandela was now more convinced than ever that peaceful protesting had run its course. He felt the struggle had reached a new stage, where violence might be necessary.[15]

SPEAR OF THE NATION

Toward the end of 1961, Mandela proposed to the ANC that they must abandon non-violence as a tactic and form a military wing, as other resistance organizations, including the PAC, were doing. The ANC and its allies eventually agreed, and wanted Mandela to start a new, separate military organization. This organization came to be known as Umkhonto we Sizwe, or "Spear of the Nation", also referred to as MK. Umkhonto we Sizwe published their stated purpose in December 1961:

> "The time comes in the life of any nation when there remain only two choices – submit or fight. That time has now come to South Africa. We shall not submit and we have no choice but to hit back by all means in our power in defence of our people, our future, and our freedom."[16]

Mandela would now be a soldier. ❖

HEADLINES: 1961–1985

Here are some major news stories from the time of Mandela's arrest and early imprisonment.

Missile Crisis in Cuba

In 1962, the world came the closest in history to a nuclear war when Premier Nikita Khrushchev of the Soviet Union attempted to put nuclear missiles in Cuba. With Cuba only 90 miles from the mainland United States, President John F. Kennedy would not allow it. Cooler heads eventually prevailed, and Khrushchev announced that Cuban installations would be destroyed and missiles returned to the Soviet Union. In return he received assurances that the United States would not invade Cuba.

Martin Luther King, Jr delivers historic speech

On 28 August 1963, Dr Martin Luther King, Jr, spoke from the steps of Washington DC's Lincoln Memorial in the United States. He delivered a speech to over 250,000 people. They had travelled there to show support for the Civil Rights Movement. In the inspirational and historic speech, King said "I have a dream that one day this nation will rise up and live out the true meaning of its creed: 'We hold these truths to be self-evident, that all men are created equal.'"

Dr Martin Luther King, Jr delivers his "I have a dream" speech in 1963.

President Kennedy assassinated

On 22 November 1963, U.S. President John F. Kennedy was fatally wounded by gunshots while riding with his wife Jacqueline in a presidential motorcade in Dallas, Texas.

Controversial pop art exhibit in New York

In 1964, Andy Warhol and other prominent pop artists displayed their art in a special exhibit in a New York art gallery. The exhibit, called "The American Supermarket", looked like just that. Warhol became famous for his consumer-driven art, such as Campbell's soup cans and Coca-Cola bottles. The exhibit had many people asking the question "What is art?" Pop artists aim to call attention to commonplace items, and to elevate them to an art-object status.

Nixon resigns

After two years of investigation of the Watergate scandal, which involved an attempt to spy on political rivals, President Richard Nixon became the first United States president to resign on 9 August 1974.

Revolution in Iran

In 1979, **revolutionaries** led by religious leader Ayatollah Khomeini established the Islamic Republic of Iran, which rejected Western influences in favour of Islamic teachings. During the revolution, hundreds of Iranians took over the U.S. embassy in Tehran and took the staff hostage. The hostages were released in January 1981, after Ronald Reagan replaced Jimmy Carter as president of the United States.

Prisoner 46664

Mandela was now underground as a revolutionary. Newspapers wrote about his disappearance, calling him the "Black Pimpernel" (see panel below). He did manage to meet up with Winnie from time to time. His friends thought he took too many risks. He was one of the most wanted men in South Africa, and he was not cautious enough. While moving from safe house to safe house, Mandela spent his time recruiting a small group to begin MK's campaign of **sabotage***. He needed outside help, though, and decided to team up with communists who had experience with explosives and fighting.*[1]

The Black Pimpernel

When Mandela was underground he was called the Black Pimpernel. This is a reference to a famous fictional character called the Scarlet Pimpernel, created by Baroness Emma Orczy. In her books, the Scarlet Pimpernel famously escapes capture during the French Revolution.

The MK's first bombing attack was on 16 December 1961. This was Dingane's Day, which commemorated the Afrikaners' massacre of Zulus in 1838. The goal was to hit government targets and avoid loss of life. Explosions went off at government offices in Johannesburg, Port Elizabeth, and Durban. One MK member was killed by his own bomb, and another lost an arm. The attacks caused minimal damage, and the explosions created only minor concern in the country. After this disappointment, the ANC leaders decided they should seek help from the rest of Africa for funding and military training. Mandela was excited to go and speak about the ANC's cause at a summit meeting in Ethiopia in February 1962. Mandela had never been outside southern Africa, and he was looking forward to his journey.[2]

MANDELA LEAVES THE COUNTRY

On 10 January 1962, Mandela said goodbye to Winnie and crossed the border to Bechuanaland, which is now Botswana. From there he flew to Tanzania. Tanzania had just become independent, and Mandela met its new president while there. He then flew to West Africa to briefly see his old friend Tambo, who was working for the ANC in exile. Mandela then flew to Ethiopia for the Pan-African Freedom Conference, where he gave a speech describing the brutal oppression of blacks by the South African government. From there he travelled further around Africa, seeking support.

From Ghana, Mandela was able to fly to London for a ten-day visit. He returned to Ethiopia in June to begin six months of military training. He would need it as leader of the MK. In the meantime, the South African government was more determined than ever to find Mandela. The police searched Winnie's house almost every day. However, the resistance leaders were planning more dramatic action in response to the government's increasingly militaristic crackdown. They telegrammed Mandela to return to South Africa to command the MK.

Cold War interests

At this time in history, the American and British governments saw the apartheid government of South Africa as an ally against the global spread of communism. Despite how they may have felt about the racist policies of apartheid, it was still a free-market system, which they felt was of more importance. For that reason, Mandela was watched by British intelligence during his travels. The British were wary of the ANC having communist sympathies, as the South African government claimed. The British kept track of potential communists and enemies of the South African state.

The British also had business interests to protect in South Africa. Activists like Mandela who threatened to overthrow the government also threatened these business interests, which were tied to the current South African government. But the British government also realized that some activists might one day actually be the new government, should apartheid come to an end. So they tried to maintain some middle ground, with an eye to the future.

CAPTURED

Mandela made it across the border, and managed to briefly see Winnie and the children, before moving on. However, on the afternoon of Sunday 5 August, Mandela's car was flagged down by armed police at a roadblock outside Howick, Natal. The authorities had apparently been tipped off about Mandela's movements and were ready for him. Even though Mandela was disguised as the chauffeur, the police knew who he was.[3] Mandela was arrested and transported to Johannesburg. He was then sentenced and held on Robben Island, the famous prison for non-whites.

RIVONIA TRIAL

Even though he was now already serving a sentence, Mandela was brought to trial again with other ANC leaders. Now began the biggest legal drama of Mandela's life, the Rivonia trial. The defendants were accused of plotting a violent campaign to overthrow the government. The trial was named after the farm where the alleged plotting took place.

As a lawyer, Mandela knew he and the defendants had little chance of winning the case. There were even documents in evidence, written in Mandela's handwriting, that spelled out plans to do exactly what he was accused of. Mandela instead had the idea that he and his colleagues would turn the court into a stage, where they would expose the cruelty of the apartheid system to the rest of the world. They also made a commitment at this point that, if they were sentenced to hang, they would go to their deaths without protest in order to shock the world into action.[4]

Mandela was his own defence lawyer. The speech he gave in his defence lasted four hours, and could not be interrupted by the rules of the trial. He spoke about his own life, from his rural tribal upbringing to the point where he finally believed that all societies should treat all races equally. Knowing they would not win their case, Mandela admitted that he and his colleagues had committed acts of sabotage and had organized an army of resistance. However, he also argued that these acts were justified because no other paths for democratic representation in the government were available.

Mandela's closing statement to the court was a perfect summary of his struggle:

> "During my lifetime I have dedicated myself to this struggle of the African people. I have fought against white domination, and I have fought against black domination. I have cherished the ideal of a democratic and free society in which all persons live together in harmony and with equal opportunities. It is an ideal which I hope to live for and to achieve. But if needs be, it is an ideal for which I am prepared to die."[5]

Predictably, the defendants were found guilty. However, because of pressure at home and abroad, including a resolution passed by the United

Nations General Assembly, the judge spared the defendants the death penalty, and instead sentenced them all to life in prison. Mandela was 46 years old when he entered the famous Robben Island Prison in 1964 and became prisoner number 46664.

CONDITIONS ON ROBBEN ISLAND

Prisoners at Robben Island spent their days doing hard labour in the stone quarry. Their cells had simple straw mats on the floor, which they slept on. The toilet of each cell was simply an iron bucket, which each prisoner had to clean out every morning. Mandela was allowed only one visitor a year, for 30 minutes. He could write and receive only one letter every six months. Some of the guards could be brutal. Beatings were not uncommon, and were often linked to what the warders (guards) saw as bad political news.

Apartheid was alive and strong at the prison, where all the guards were white. Mandela quickly found that black prisoners were targeted for

The history of Robben Island

Since the Dutch settled in the Cape in the 17th century, Robben Island has mostly been used as a prison. Before the anti-apartheid activists were imprisoned there, others felt its isolation, including Xhosa chiefs whose stories Mandela knew well. Muslim leaders from Indonesia, Dutch and British soldiers, and even civilian men and women had also been imprisoned on Robben Island.

The island has had other uses. In 1846–1931 it was used as a hospital for people with leprosy, as well as for the mentally and chronically ill. It was still also used as a prison at that time, housing minor criminals and political prisoners. During World War II (1939–1945), it was a training and defence station. Since 1997, Robben Island has been a museum and heritage site.

unfair treatment. He and his fellow inmates planned to continue their campaign of resistance, even in prison. Black inmates at the prison were given short trousers, no matter how cold the weather got. The rest of the inmates were given long trousers. This would be Mandela's first issue.

Soon after arriving, Mandela demanded to see the head of the prison in a protest against the short trousers. Mandela continued to argue his case for two weeks. Finally the prison commander gave in, and Mandela found a pair of long trousers on his cell floor one day. However, when he found out that he was the only black prisoner who had been given long trousers, he refused to wear them. Mandela continued to argue his point, until all inmates were finally offered long trousers. Mandela could see that his gifts of intelligence, charm, dignity, and persuasion could give him a sense of control, even within the notorious prison.

Mandela's mother died of a heart attack in 1968, and his oldest son died in a car crash the next year. Mandela was not allowed to attend the funerals. Prisoners on Robben Island were cut off from the outside world. They were not allowed newspapers or magazines, and could not listen to the radio or watch television. But they craved news. The inmates tried to follow events by gathering up the scraps of newspaper the guards used to wrap their food. Every new prisoner was also welcome, because he would bring news of the latest happenings.

The routine went on at Robben Island as years passed. There were continuous challenges to the apartheid government of South Africa. There were strikes and protests, as well as more violent acts of sabotage. When authorities violently stopped protests, it would simply bring more protests. International pressure on the oppressive authorities was growing. The inmates understood this pressure, and they protested from within the prison. They would sometimes go on hunger strikes and refuse to eat for days. They knew that if a well-known political prisoner like Mandela were allowed to die, the apartheid authorities would be weakened in the face of international outrage.[6]

Clever communications

Prisoners were not usually allowed to talk to one another. However, they found opportunities when they could, such as while cleaning their toilet buckets first thing in the morning, when the guards stayed away to avoid the smell. They were also able to talk very quietly at night sometimes. According to Mandela:

"The acoustics along the corridor were quite good, and we would try to chat a bit to each other before going to sleep. The warder would walk up and down a few times to make sure we were not reading or writing. After a few months, we would sprinkle a handful of sand along the corridor so that we could hear the warder's footsteps and have time to stop talking or hide any contraband. Only when we were quiet did he take a seat in the small office at the end of the passage where he dozed until morning."[7]

A PERSUASIVE MAN

New protests in South Africa meant new government crackdowns, which meant new prisoners on Robben Island. The new prisoners were usually younger and more militant than Mandela and his ANC friends. They rejected cooperation with whites and other non-black Africans. Mandela admired their courage, and they often reminded him of himself at a younger age. He also saw that their energy could be very valuable politically.[8]

Mandela used his gifts of reason, patience, and charm to win many young leaders over to his point of view. The challenge of charming people, slowly wearing them down, and finally convincing them of the ANC point of view taught Mandela even more patience and tolerance, and it helped prepare him and his colleagues for negotiations they would later face. The confinement of Robben Island allowed political rivals to find common ground that they never could on the outside. Robben Island became something of a political melting pot of future leaders, who would often become lifelong friends.

A cell in the Robben Island prison.

Realizing they had some power on the island, inmates continued to protest. Over the years, the prisoners slowly and patiently gained better conditions and more freedoms. Mandela also came to realize that even in a brutal place like Robben Island, there could be human compassion from surprising sources. Certain white guards were sympathetic to the prisoners, and they sometimes smuggled in newspapers and gave out extra food. Mandela's philosophy of not judging by race grew as he witnessed these kindnesses.

Mandela's charm affected some of the white prison warders, and he became friends with James Gregory, a white prison guard. In fact, Gregory enjoyed Mandela's company so much that he later said that he retired as a prison guard because he was bored after Mandela was freed.

James Gregory was invited to Mandela's presidential inauguration in 1994 as an honoured guest.[9]

UNIVERSITY OF ROBBEN ISLAND

As the inmates were given more freedoms, the combination of younger political activists and older intellectuals like Mandela made Robben Island feel more like an academy for future leaders than a prison. Inmates were allowed to speak more freely, were allowed access to books, and were even allowed to plant a garden in the courtyard. Prisoners with degrees took turns teaching various subjects to other inmates, even while working. Soon, as conditions further improved, even the work at the lime quarry was halted. Prisoners moved around freely, talking in groups. They spent most of the day out of their cells, in the courtyard. They even made a tennis court.

By the 1970s, the atmosphere was such that the prison came to be called the University of Robben Island. The isolation of the prison made continuous study possible, and it was a welcome distraction. Many inmates who were illiterate learned to read and write. Many prisoners were even motivated to learn more through correspondence schools (through the post). Several were barely educated when they arrived, but left prison with one or more degrees.

Family sacrifices

Mandela was allowed half an hour visit from Winnie in 1964, and then another two years later. She was arrested in 1969. After her release, Winnie was eventually allowed to visit again in December 1975, and she brought their two daughters. Mandela had not seen his daughter Zindzi since she was three, and he was now surprised, at age 15, by how much she resembled her mother. Mandela painfully recognized that he had sacrificed being a good father for the ANC's cause.[10]

> *"He always had some remorse about the fact that he could never be the kind of father that he wanted to be."*[11]
> —Neville Alexander, a political activist imprisoned with Mandela on Robben Island

WINNIE'S TROUBLES

Winnie and Mandela were both tied to their passion for politics. Winnie had been arrested while Mandela was in jail, and then banned from leaving Johannesburg. She had also been banned from political activity, but she couldn't stay away from it. The government was determined to get her and had spies watching at all times. She was finally arrested at dawn on 12 May 1969, and taken away while her children cried. When her lawyer came to visit, Winnie hadn't been allowed to wash for 200 days. She later spent time in the prison hospital for malnutrition.

Winnie was finally released after 17 months in solitary confinement. Some of her acquaintances thought the experience had changed her; made her bitter and a bit mad.[12] She became more aggressive after that, and remained politically active. She was in the thick of the Soweto revolt of 1976, which brought international attention to the oppressive situation in South Africa. As time went on, Winnie became increasingly involved with young radicals and violent protest. She even started to encourage violent acts.

In 1975, the Minister of Education declared that some classes must be taught in Afrikaans, a language similar to Dutch and used by South African whites. Many felt that black childrens' education would suffer because they were not being taught in their native language. On 16 June 1976, students marched in protest in Soweto, a township outside of Johannesburg. The police fired on the crowd, killing children. This led to violence all across the country.

16 June 1976: Black students in Soweto charge in protest of the compulsory teaching of Afrikaans in schools. The police used tear gas, then opened fire on the crowd, which was estimated to number 10,000.

> ## "Only free men can negotiate. Prisoners cannot enter into contracts.... I cannot and will not give any undertaking at a time when I and you, the people, are not free."
> —Excerpt from Mandela's refusal to accept conditional freedom

Sports vs apartheid

Internationally, South Africa excelled in many sports. However, as anti-apartheid sentiment grew around the world, it led to sports boycotts of the country. In 1970, South Africa was formally expelled from the International Olympic Committee. In 1976, after police shot and killed unarmed protestors, football's world body FIFA expelled the white Football Association of South Africa. Eventually, anti-apartheid activists worldwide rallied around an international sports boycott of South Africa as a form of resistance.

BECOMING A CELEBRITY

Mandela's 60th birthday was celebrated around the world on 18 July 1978. He had become a celebrity. By the early 1980s, Mandela was probably the world's most famous political prisoner. The Free Mandela campaign, begun in 1980, soon had many supporters around the world. In 1982, after 18 years on Robben Island, Mandela was transferred to Pollsmoor prison, on the mainland. It seemed luxurious in some ways, but the isolation also had its drawbacks compared to the **camaraderie** shared on Robben Island. However, the transfer was a sign that the South African government was feeling more pressure, both at home and abroad.

In 1983 and 1984, it was clear that Prime Minister Botha's attempts to extend segregation and weaken the ANC were backfiring. An insurrection that started around Johannesburg quickly spread across the country. The government could not contain the outbursts, and had to call in troops to control townships. It seemed like the apartheid government was losing its ability to govern and maintain control.

MK actions

Once Mandela was arrested, the MK, or Umkhonto we Sizwe, was without a leader. The rest of the MK and ANC leadership decided to move the armed struggle abroad in order to prepare with military training. MK guerrillas trained in camps outside South Africa, with hopes that they would then return with the skills necessary for the revolution. The MK saw little success, however, and had still not fired a single shot within South Africa's borders by 1976. However, the Soweto Uprising that year led many young black men and women to cross the border seeking military training with the MK. After the government's brutality, they were eager to strike a blow against apartheid.

With new recruits and support, the 1980s would bring more successful actions for the MK. In 1983, the MK detonated what became known as the Church Street bomb near the South African Air Force headquarters. There were 19 deaths, and 217 were injured. Some victims were military, but many were civilians. The MK conducted a series of bombings in South Africa over the next ten years.

FREE MANDELA CAMPAIGN

The Free Mandela campaign climaxed in the mid-1980s. There were large anti-apartheid rallies and protests in New York, Washington DC, and other cities around the world. Famous musicians including Bruce Springsteen and Miles Davis released an anti-apartheid album. In the United Kingdom, the song "Free Mandela" reached the Top Ten on music charts. The strong feelings felt by people around the world were also having an impact on business in South Africa.

With pressure from outside, and protests and violence increasing within the country, South Africa's President Botha felt he had to try something. On 31 January 1985, Botha offered Mandela his freedom, but only if he rejected violence as a political weapon. Botha thought that he might corner Mandela. If he refused to renounce violence, the outside world would come to understand that Mandela deserved to be in prison.

Mandela began a response immediately that same evening. He would not be a pawn for the apartheid government to look good internationally when he could feel that they were crumbling. He carefully wrote a speech that rejected the government's offer while keeping the option of negotiation open. He also stressed the unity and determination of the ANC. Mandela gave the speech to Winnie when she next visited him. On 10 February, Mandela's daughter Zindzi read his speech to a huge, packed stadium near Johannesburg. ❖

Mandela's refusal

"Let him [Botha] renounce violence. Let him say that he will dismantle apartheid … Let him free all who have been imprisoned, banished, or exiled for their opposition to apartheid. Let him guarantee free political activity so that people may decide who will govern them … I cherish my own freedom dearly, but I care even more for your freedom … Only free men can negotiate. Prisoners cannot enter into contracts … I cannot and will not give any undertaking at a time when I and you, the people, are not free. Your freedom and mine cannot be separated …"[13]

Headlines: 1985–1994

Here are some major news stories from the time of Mandela's freedom and campaigning.

Chinese students' rally for democracy turns deadly

Tens of thousands of Chinese students gathered in Beijing's Tiananmen Square on 19 April 1989, to show support for a democratic government. They occupied the square for seven weeks. As the days passed during that time, millions of people joined in, calling for reform.

On 3 June the government decided to put an end to the protest. It sent tanks and the military, which fired randomly on the unarmed students. The number of deaths is not known, but estimates say it could be several hundred. The ferocity of the attack took people by surprise and was condemned by leaders around the world, including U.S. President George H. W. Bush and British Prime Minister Margaret Thatcher.

Hubble Space Telescope launched

The Hubble Space Telescope was launched on 24 April 1990, in order to explore space. The telescope is in orbit around the Earth, controlled by computers. Once it was in orbit, Hubble took pictures that no other camera or telescope on Earth could take. It has helped astronomers learn important information about our solar system.

Soviet Union dissolves: Cold War over!

The Soviet Union was declared officially dissolved on 25 December 1991. As one of the two main powers involved, the collapse of the Soviet Union meant an end to the Cold War.

A refugee camp in Rwanda, in the wake of the genocide.

Genocide in Rwanda: 800,000 dead

Rwanda is a country in Africa of 7 million people. It is comprised of two main ethnic groups: the Tutsis and the Hutus. The two groups have been at war for control of their country since 1962. In 1994, the Hutu militia killed 800,000 Tutsis, an estimated 10,000 a day. Tutsi forces invading from other countries were finally able to stop the Hutus, but not before 10 percent of the population of Rwanda was killed.

A free man

*Late in February of 1985, it was determined that Mandela needed surgery for an enlarged **prostate gland**. Everyone watched South Africa anxiously until Mandela was safely recovering. Many thought that, should Mandela die while in custody, the country would descend into chaos once and for all. The worldwide commotion caused by Mandela's illness created more outside pressure on the South African government.*

By July of 1985, law and order had virtually broken down in the townships of South Africa. On 20 July, the government again declared a state of emergency. The activists did not back down, and the battles in townships attracted international news coverage. The harsh government response and violence seen on television sets around the world was the tipping point. The international community was becoming more determined than ever to isolate apartheid South Africa in order to bring about reform in that country and an end to apartheid policies.

Anti-apartheid protesters were pressuring international banks to stop doing business in South Africa. The pressure worked, and in 1985, some major banks called in loans and refused to renew their credit to the South African Reserve Bank. Chase Manhattan cut its links with South Africa that year, and the value of the South African rand dropped by 35 percent. The Johannesburg Stock Exchange was forced to close for four days that same year (1985). In August of 1986, the U.S. Senate Foreign Relations

There were many small, local gestures around the world to show support for Mandela and the Free Mandela movement. Streets were renamed for Mandela, and "Free Mandela" graffiti appeared in cities around the world. In Leeds, Mandela Gardens was opened in 1982, and when scientists at Leeds University discovered a new fragment of matter in the 1980s, they named it the Mandela Particle.

Committee voted for strict economic **sanctions** against South Africa. Other countries did the same. Major companies around the world began closing down operations within the country, and investors were losing confidence in President Botha.

SECRET NEGOTIATIONS

After his operation, Mandela was moved into new quarters, away from his fellow inmates. Mandela was optimistic, however, and rightly so. Minister of Justice Kobie Coetsee secretly approached Mandela on behalf of the government to see if he would negotiate on behalf of his resistance colleagues. Even though he knew his friends, the other leaders of the ANC, would be furious, Mandela decided he would negotiate with the government on his own, in secret. He felt that the government must have realized that the turning point had come, and their apartheid regime would not last much longer.

It would take five years for the government to convince Mandela to do business, however. It was a lonely period in Mandela's life, sectioned off by himself and facing the government alone. Eventually, Mandela told some of his ANC friends about his negotiations. The reactions were heated, and there were rumours that Mandela had sold out to the government. But Mandela felt he must be strong and carry on. His old friend Tambo trusted him and tried to hold the ANC and its allies together from the outside.[1]

On 9 December 1988, Mandela was driven to Victor Verster prison, his new living quarters. This time, however, he was taken to a warden's house, with a spacious garden, modern bathrooms, a high-tech kitchen, and even a swimming pool. Mandela was very comfortable, but he was even more cut off from his friends and colleagues. He knew now, however, that his freedom was near.[2]

His optimism was tempered with some bad news about Winnie. That same month, four boys rumoured to be spies were abducted by members of the Mandela United Football Club. This was a group of young men who acted as Winnie's bodyguards and operated out of her home. They wore the clothes of a football team, but were known to act like thugs

Freedomfest

On 11 June 1988, on the 24th anniversary of Mandela's imprisonment, a rock concert called "Freedomfest" was held outside London to celebrate Mandela's 70th birthday. An audience of 72,000 attended, and it was televised in 60 countries, with millions of viewers. Performers included Sting, Peter Gabriel, George Michael, the Eurythmics, Al Green, the Bee Gees, and others.

around the neighbourhood. The boys were beaten inside Winnie's home. Three escaped, but the battered body of 13-year-old Stompie Seipei was found weeks later. Winnie, who was now known for her endorsement of violence, was implicated in the incident, and was charged with kidnapping and assault. The ANC was appalled. But she was Mandela's famous wife, and they tried to help and control Winnie. Mandela's love for her and sympathy for what she had gone through in his absence kept him loyal to Winnie.[3]

DE KLERK BECOMES PRESIDENT

In August 1989, Botha resigned as president of South Africa after suffering a stroke. F. W. de Klerk was sworn in as the president. Mandela continued negotiations with the government, and it seemed like he was now calling the shots. Mandela called on de Klerk to release political prisoners, including his friends Sisulu and Kathrada, whom he thought would not cause violence once outside. The government released eight prisoners, including Sisulu and Kathrada.

By 1990, Mandela was the only major opposition leader left in prison. This helped reinforce his position of leadership and authority among the opposition. After all, it would be hard for his people to accuse Mandela of betraying them when he had spent more time in jail than anyone else. Mandela watched closely as President de Klerk continued to make concessions (back down). He allowed a large protest march to take place in Cape Town without police interference. He did away with segregated beaches, parks, bathrooms, and restaurants.

The Berlin Wall had come down in November of 1989, and the Cold War was cooling off. Western powers no longer saw the communist influence among the opposition in South Africa as a threat, and the South African apartheid government was losing even more ground internationally. De Klerk felt he must act quickly and boldly.

De Klerk finally agreed to Mandela's request for a direct meeting.

Mandela insisted that there should be no preconditions for the meeting. The two met on 13 December 1989. The National Party of de Klerk was pushing the idea of "group rights" at this time, which focused on each racial group of South Africa individually, where a separation of the races would still be the rule. Mandela expressed that the world would see through this as yet another attempt to extend apartheid. When the meeting was over, de Klerk had made no promises. However, Mandela left the meeting feeling hopeful. He thought that de Klerk might really be different from his predecessors, and seriously willing to find an agreeable solution.[4]

"When asked what role I would play in the organization, I told the press that I would play whatever role the ANC ordered."
—Nelson Mandela

Mandela's "prison" could barely be called that at this point. It looked more like the office of the head of the ANC! Mandela was now free to have visitors, including politicians. Leaders and academics were frequently visiting the house. Some in the movement who saw his luxurious accommodations again worried that Mandela was "selling out".[5] However, he was careful to leak certain memos to reassure colleagues that he had made no commitments to the government. All of his statements and talks made it clear that Mandela was still a loyal member of the ANC, determined to keep them united.

THE TURNING POINT

By 1990, the situation in South Africa was getting worse for the government. Pressures from abroad were continuing to build, and the

South African economy was in a serious crisis. Boycotts and economic sanctions continued. If de Klerk released Mandela, some economic sanctions would go away. During the month of January, de Klerk prepared a speech to give at the opening of the South African parliament in February.

At last parliament assembled for the speech on 2 February 1990. Members of parliament were stunned as de Klerk reversed the policies of over 30 years of South African government in a matter of a few minutes. He announced that all political prisoners not guilty of violent crimes would be released. All executions would be suspended. Outlawed

F. W. de Klerk's moment

Frederik Willem de Klerk had a long history in the conservative politics of the National Party. It was not surprising when he replaced P. W. Botha as president in 1989. However, de Klerk's first speech was a surprise. In that speech, he called for a non-racist South Africa and for negotiations about the country's future. With that speech, de Klerk began the end of apartheid. De Klerk and others could see that apartheid was coming to an end one way or another. Only by being on the right side of history could de Klerk and the white government hope to manage a smooth transition. The situation was urgent. Social order was breaking down around the country. The government could potentially lose control.

By participating in the transition to a new government, de Klerk could ease the fears of the white minority. Whites were worried they would find themselves governed by the black majority they had oppressed for so many years, and that it could turn into violent revenge. It was clear that Mandela would likely be the new leader when a reformed South African government emerged, so a lot was resting on him. People relaxed once they realized Mandela was forgiving and not bitter over his suffering. Despite how the media had built up Mandela as a larger-than-life figure, he actually seemed to live up to those expectations. De Klerk also had to ease the concerns of those doing business in South Africa. Once it was clear Mandela was not a communist, Western countries became less worried that their economic interests would be harmed.

anti-apartheid political organizations, including the ANC and even the South African Communist Party, would no longer be banned. The heavy police control of black townships would end. And, de Klerk said, the government would release its most famous prisoner, Nelson Mandela, without conditions.

MANDELA IS FREE!

South Africa suddenly felt like a new country. The ANC was now an important, above-ground political organization. On 10 February 1990, de Klerk informed Mandela he would be released the very next day. Mandela was distressed that he had such short notice, and that he did not have a chance to say goodbye to the prison staff.[6] But de Klerk would not delay his release any longer. At the age of 71, after 27 years in jail, Mandela walked out a free man on 11 February 1990. Journalists and television crews were there to capture the moment. By this time, the legend of Mandela had taken on a life of its own, and pictures of Mandela had been banned for years. No one knew quite what to expect. When he finally emerged, Mandela was welcomed by a large crowd. It was a powerful image for the world, and a slightly startling moment for Mandela, who had not expected such a scene. He later described it:

> "I saw a tremendous commotion and a great crowd of people: hundreds of photographers and television cameras and newspeople as well as several thousand well-wishers. I was astounded and a little bit alarmed."[7]

Mandela was scheduled to hold a press conference the afternoon after his release. He was not used to so many journalists and cameras, but he now had specific things he wanted to say. He again wanted to proclaim his loyalty to the ANC, and he later reflected that "at every turn I sought to reassure them. When asked what role I would play in the organization, I told the press that I would play whatever role the ANC ordered."[8]

Mandela was now free to travel. He had seen very little of the world

A crowd outside of Nelson Mandela's Soweto home celebrates and waits for his arrival, after hearing the news of his release from prison.

and felt he had a lot of catching up to do. Mandela went abroad for two main political reasons. He used his reputation to raise support and money for the ANC, and he worked to promote a continuation of the sanctions against apartheid South Africa. Mandela understood the effect economic sanctions had had in bringing the National Party government to the negotiating table, and he did not want that pressure to be reduced until apartheid was completely gone.

In his travels, Mandela met with British Prime Minister Margaret Thatcher, Canadian Prime Minister Brian Mulroney, U.S. President George H. W. Bush, and French President François Mitterrand. He addressed the United States Congress and spoke before Canada's Parliament. On a visit to New York City, Mandela addressed the United Nations, and he was cheered by a million people as he rode in a car up Broadway. Mandela attended a huge concert at Wembley Stadium in London, where international stars such as Lou Reed, Neil Young, Patti LaBelle, and Tracy Chapman performed for 75,000 young people. Mandela also visited Zambia, Zimbabwe, Namibia, Algeria, Sweden, and Ireland on his travels. He kept a busy and tiring schedule. The fight was not yet over.

Though he was now free, Mandela was still wary of the government attempting to manipulate him in negotiations against his friends. One of the first things he did was express his undying loyalty to the ANC and a need for the struggle to continue until apartheid was gone. At first he seemed to be calling for a continuation of the armed struggle. However, this was a calculated move on Mandela's part to strengthen his position in negotiations with the government. Without the backing of the ANC and people in that movement, Mandela knew he could be brushed aside. He needed to make it clear that he was negotiating with their support. It quickly became clear Mandela did not want violence.

As spokesman for the ANC, Mandela knew that he had to try to calm the people. A few days after his release, Mandela spoke at a Soweto stadium filled with 100,000 people. He asked students to return to school and pleaded for less crime. He said there could be no freedom for Africans without there first being civility and peace. In May 1990, the ANC and National Party government began negotiations.[9]

Since Mandela had returned home, he had faced a private struggle on top of his public pressures. He and Winnie had grown apart during their long separation. When they were together again, this became apparent to them both. In February of 1991, Winnie's trial began. Mandela stood by his wife and attended the trial. He asked friends to show their support as well, and many did. Winnie was also a popular celebrity and political figure in her own right.

When the verdict came, Winnie was found guilty of kidnapping and accessory to assault and sentenced to six years in prison. Her conviction

Inkatha Freedom Party (IFP)

The Inkatha Freedom Party is a Zulu nationalist political party. In 1975, Zulu Chief Buthelezi began appealing to Zulu nationalism and growing his support among Zulus. Inkatha's original goal was to restore the Zulu kingdom and the land the Zulus lost due to European colonization. The relationship between the ANC and IFP deteriorated as the IFP cooperated with the apartheid government in some cases. The IFP also began carrying out violent attacks on members of rival political parties, including the ANC. Inkatha's violent acts were encouraged and secretly supported by the state police. Since the first free elections in 1994, the Inkatha Freedom Party has steadily lost support. In the 2004 election, the IFP even lost control of the native Zulu province of KwaZulu-Natal to the ANC.

was reduced to only kidnapping and was suspended after an appeal, and she only paid a fine. But certain witnesses later changed their stories and said she was guilty. Her reputation suffered. She was losing her political following and the support of the ANC. Mandela still loved Winnie, but he disagreed with her extreme views. It also seemed that she no longer wanted to be with him. She became more openly defiant, and eventually he could not ignore that the marriage had failed. On 13 April 1992, Mandela announced that he and Winnie were separating. It was very difficult for Mandela to express his private sadness so publicly.[10]

VIOLENCE AND VICTORY

Violence continued as negotiations stopped and started again over the next months and years. The worst violence was between supporters of the ANC, which claimed to represent all South Africans, and Zulu Chief Buthelezi's Inkatha Freedom Party, which believed only it could represent the Zulus in KwaZulu-Natal. Mandela and the ANC broke off negotiations with de Klerk at one point because they believed the

Inkatha violence against the ANC was being encouraged by the white government. It was later found that this was true. However, at this time, as the death toll increased towards the end of 1992, Mandela and de Klerk were both concerned enough to go back to the negotiating table.

In September 1992, Mandela and de Klerk signed the Record of Understanding, which promised formal investigations into the violence and police actions around the country. It also established an elected constitutional assembly. That elected assembly would write a new constitution for the country. Throughout 1993, Mandela continued to press for peace. After a popular ANC leader was assassinated in April, Mandela was successful in urging calm and was able to prevent further violence. Mandela and de Klerk were internationally praised for their efforts, and in December 1993, they were jointly awarded the Nobel Peace Prize.

In June 1993, a meeting of 26 political parties set the date of 27 April 1994, for what would be the first fully representative democratic election in South Africa. All races would finally be allowed to vote. In order to make it happen, both sides had to compromise and cut a deal. In exchange for allowing a one-person, one-vote democratic election, the ANC would give up its ideas of **nationalizing** business. The blacks would gain political control, but the whites would be allowed to keep economic power. A non-white, ANC government would not confiscate (seize, or take) the property and businesses of whites, though blacks could now compete on a level playing field.

There was more violence leading up to the election. In March 1994, Inkatha members, secretly encouraged by the government, killed 53 people while trying to sabotage the election. Mandela and others were worried about what might happen during the actual election. Given the tension and violence of the recent past, would things turn chaotic, or would calm and order prevail? When the voting finally happened in April, almost 20 million South Africans voted. There were no violent incidents on the polling days. The vote was by party, and the ANC received 63 percent of the votes, the National Party 20 percent, and the Zulu Inkatha party 11 percent. Mandela was elected president, and the ANC won 252 out of 400 seats in the national assembly. It was an overwhelming victory for the ANC. Just over four years earlier, Mandela had been serving a life sentence in prison. Now, on 10 May 1994, he was sworn in as president of a united country.

Mandela's election and inauguration were reported around the world as a triumph of the better part of the human spirit. It was the final fulfillment of the legend of Mandela the press had built up around the world. However, while the outside world may have seen this as the perfect end to the story, Mandela's work with this new challenge was just beginning. It would not be easy to rebuild a country that had been torn apart by apartheid for so many years. ❖

31 January 1994: Nelson Mandela greets a supportive crowd as he launches his presidential campaign.

HEADLINES: 1995–1999

Here are some major news stories from Mandela's time as president.

Tibetan freedom concert

To support the international movement to gain freedom for Tibet from China, a fundraising concert was held in San Francisco in 1995. The hip hop group Beastie Boys and the Milarepa Fund organized the concert to raise funds for and awareness of the issue. Performers included Beastie Boys, Red Hot Chili Peppers, Rage Against the Machine, and De La Soul. One hundred thousand attended, and it raised over 800,000 U.S. dollars.

The Beastie Boys, performing at the Tibetan Freedom Concert.

Rabin assassinated

The prime minister of Israel, Yitzhak Rabin, was assassinated on 4 November 1995. Rabin was the first native-born Israeli prime minister. He had a record as an Israeli war hero, which allowed him to overcome divisive politics in order to sign the Oslo peace agreement with the Palestinians. The Oslo Accords marked the first face-to-face agreement between Israel and political representatives of the Palestinians. It was meant to be a framework for relations between Israel and a future Palestinian state. Yigal Amir said he shot the prime minister because he opposed Rabin's signing of the Oslo Accords. Yitzhak Rabin won the Nobel Prize for Peace in 1994, along with Yasser Arafat and Shimon Peres, for their work to bring peace to their region, the Middle East. Since Rabin's assassination, the peace process has faced numerous setbacks.

First novel in Harry Potter series published

In 1997, author J. K. Rowling published the first in her series of books about Harry Potter. The book centred around a young boy who discovers that he is a wizard. His adventures in the wizarding world captivated children and adults everywhere, and have encouraged children to read.

Hong Kong is returned to China

On 1 July 1997, British control ended in Hong Kong, and it was given back to Chinese rule.

Yugoslavia dissolves

Continuous wars between 1991 and 1995 led to the break-up of Yugoslavia. Conflicts increased and there was evidence of genocide. NATO began a military campaign, and control of Kosovo was handed to the United Nations in 1999.

President of a new South Africa

*Mandela said when he went into office "We have no experience of elections, of **parliamentary** practice, and of state administration."[1] He was only out of prison for four years when he gained the presidency. He had spent 27 years in jail. But he and his fellow ANC members were determined to prove to South Africa and the world that they could govern successfully.*

However, no one could be sure how white people would react to a black leader. In other countries in similar situations, white people in powerful and essential positions had been unsupportive of the new, black, leaders, and the governments had struggled. Mandela knew that he needed the support of all people in order to rebuild the nation. His struggle began by getting the **cabinet** to work together. It was made up of ANC members, Afrikaners, and National Party members. Despite the fact that the cabinet members all had very different beliefs, they were able to work together, and committed to making the government successful.

President Mandela had many challenges facing him when he took office. The first important task that he and his cabinet had to complete was the writing of a new constitution. They worked day and night. When the copies were released, not everyone was satisfied with the outcome. However, all seemed to agree it was better than what had been in place. It was ratified (confirmed by formal approval) by the cabinet in October 1996, and signed into law by Mandela in December. The new government had many other plans and hopes. The problem was that South Africa did not have much money. Foreign investors who had made a great deal of money during the years of apartheid now pulled their money out of South Africa, fearing unrest. Mandela tried to convince other countries to invest in South Africa, but none seemed willing to believe that the country was now stable.

After the first year of Mandela's term, not much had changed for the black citizens of South Africa. They were expecting houses for the homeless, working sewers, better schools for their children. The problem was that there was just no money to do these things. The government had to spend much of the first year building a structure, so that when they did put programs in place, they would not have to borrow money, and the programs could be stable. While this happened, people still suffered, often without easily available clean water and no electricity. Because they did not have these services, many people refused to pay their bills.

Nuclear state

In March 1993, de Klerk announced that South Africa had built six atomic bombs in secret prior to 1991, when it signed the Nuclear Non-proliferation Treaty. De Klerk said the bombs had been dismantled and destroyed prior to the signing of the treaty. South Africa was the first nation to reject nuclear weapons after having had them.

The Nuclear Non-proliferation Treaty (NPT) was signed in 1968. Its main goal is to prevent the spread of nuclear weapons and weapons technology. Its other elements include promoting co-operation in the peaceful uses of nuclear energy, and a goal of achieving nuclear disarmament. A total of 187 parties have signed the treaty.

SOME UNITY AND PROGRESS

The Masakhane Campaign was launched by the government in 1995. Masakhane is a Zulu word that means "let us build together". The government needed to make it clear to people in South Africa that everyone had to work together to make South Africa a better place. Everyone had to do their part in order for the country to be successful; if people wanted to receive better service from the government, they needed to pay their bills. The Masakhane Campaign also focused on building community pride and a sense of **civic** duty.

When the time came for Mandela's 1996 State of the Nation address, many improvements were in place for South Africans that were not there before. In his speech he spoke of hundreds of thousands of people who had access to clean drinking water, hundreds of thousands of homes with electricity that had been built, free medical care, free education, a clinic-building program, a health system, and the fact that there were many people who now felt secure in ownership of their land. Mandela was determined to change life for the better for South Africans.[2]

"He symbolizes a much broader forgiveness and understanding and reaching out... sending the message of what he thought was the best way to save lives in this country, to bring reconciliation...."
— Graca Machel

Mandela needed to find a way to unite all of the people of South Africa. They had lived for far too long under apartheid and segregation. He especially needed to reach out to white people, who had been fearful of what he would do when he became president. He needed to reassure

24 June 1995: South African President Nelson Mandela congratulates François Pienaar of the country's national Springbok rugby team. Mandela wore the Springbok jersey as he presented Pienaar with the World Cup trophy.

them that he did not want to punish anyone for the past, and he needed to bring black people and white people together.

Rugby was a very popular sport among white people in South Africa at the time, and was disliked by most black people. In fact, many black people went to the South African national team's games to root for the other team. Mandela went on a crusade to convince all people to support the Springboks, South Africa's team. He wanted everyone to cheer for them in the World Cup that would be hosted in South Africa in 1995. He worked hard, and won over people to the game. In an exciting and almost unbelievable game, the Springboks won. To this day, the image of Nelson Mandela handing the trophy to the white Afrikaner François Pienaar is a symbol to many of the end of apartheid.

Bishop Desmond Tutu (1931–)

Bishop Desmond Tutu was born in 1931 in the Transvaal in South Africa. He graduated from the University of South Africa in 1954 and worked for three years as a high school teacher. He then studied theology and was ordained as a priest in 1960. In 1984, Bishop Tutu was awarded the Nobel Peace Prize for his efforts in crusading for racial justice in South Africa. In 1996, he was appointed by President Nelson Mandela to chair the Truth and Reconciliation Commission. Bishop Desmond Tutu has remained active since the presentation of the Commission's report in 1998, writing books and acting as visiting professor at various universities.

TRUTH AND RECONCILIATION

In July 1995, the president passed the Promotion of National Unity and **Reconciliation** Act. The act provided for the creation of a Truth and Reconciliation Commission. The Commission, with Desmond Tutu as chair, had four main objectives: to discover and explain the human rights violations from 1960 to 1994, to grant **amnesty** to people who disclosed their human rights crimes, to make known the fate of victims or to let living victims tell their stories, and to compile a report of the findings.

The Commission asked people to send them their stories. Thousands of statements from victims and perpetrators, or people responsible for violent and criminal acts, were sent. **Hearings** were held, many open to the public, and people came to speak before the committee. Victims spoke of the violence they had lived through. Perpetrators spoke of the crimes they had committed. The hearings were very emotional.

Dozens of hearings were held in cities and rural communities. Anyone who declined to apply for amnesty with the Commission could still be prosecuted later under the law. This encouraged participation, which meant the truth was more likely to come out. Many people felt the hearings would help heal the nation for that reason. Even if people did not serve time in jail, they were at least forced to face the people they wronged or their families. The truth would be known, and there would be some sense of closure concerning the past. However, other people criticized the Commission. Many people were unhappy with the fact that those who had committed crimes would not be punished.[3] However, for many more it was a chance to forgive, or ask for forgiveness, and to learn the truth. It was a chance to begin a healing process and move on as a more united country.

The Commission published a report of its findings. The primary finding was that most of the human rights violations were perpetrated by the South African government and their law enforcement agencies. The Commission found that these groups were not the only ones to blame; the report stated that even though the ANC contended that they acted in self-defence, they contributed to the violence in the years 1990–1994. Other political parties, such as the Inkatha Freedom Party, and leaders, such as P. W. Botha, were found to be guilty of human rights violations as well.[4]

The degree to which the Truth and Reconciliation Commission was accepted by the country was perhaps dependent on how Mandela handled things. As president of the country, Mandela backed the Commission's report and took responsibility for setting up the process. He felt truth, forgiveness, and unity were the most important things South Africa needed for its future. Mandela's future wife Graca Machel believed Mandela played a crucial role in the nation's healing:

> "He symbolizes a much broader forgiveness and understanding and reaching out ... So his role is not to be underestimated too. He knew exactly the way he wanted to come out, but also the way he addressed the people from the beginning, sending the message of what he thought was the best way to save lives in this country, to bring reconciliation ..."[5]

INTERNATIONAL RELATIONS

Mandela not only had to heal his country at home, he also had to repair South Africa's damaged reputation in the world. He travelled to other countries, meeting with world leaders to assure them South Africa was moving past its problems. He immediately restored **diplomatic** relations with many countries that had previously shunned South Africa due to its policy of apartheid. In his first year as president, all United Nations sanctions against South Africa were lifted. Many countries pledged monetary support to help rebuild South Africa. However, it was not enough to help the struggling nation.

International relations were very good for South Africa. Nelson Mandela was the perfect choice as statesman and spokesperson for the country. He visited many countries during his time in office. He was a symbol of

6 October 1994: South African President Nelson Mandela, during an address to the U.S. Congress.

freedom to everyone around the world, not just in South Africa. All the United Nations sanctions were lifted. South Africa again became part of the Commonwealth of Nations.

He became involved in world issues, often giving opinions and speaking out if he felt the need. One case he was famously involved in was the case of an American plane that was bombed over Lockerbie, Scotland, in 1988. Agents from the country of Libya were blamed. The United States demanded that the Libyan suspects be taken out of Libya and brought to trial. Mandela and South Africa had a good relationship with Libya and its leader, Muammar Quadaffi. Mandela insisted that the Libyans be tried in a neutral country. The president of the United States, George H. W. Bush, was angered by this. He became even angrier when Mandela went ahead with a visit to Libya that had been planned before the bombing.

Mandela said that no country should tell him who his friends could be. After his visit to Libya, he travelled to a Commonwealth Summit in Edinburgh, Scotland. There he argued again that the suspects should be tried in a neutral place. He was able to earn the support of British families of the victims of the bombings. Mandela eventually helped to make a deal: Libya would give up the suspects, and in return, the United Nations would drop all sanctions against them. The trial would be held under Scottish law, but in the Netherlands. It was proof of Mandela's political power and ability to find solutions to difficult problems.

MARRIAGE TO GRACA

During his term as president, Mandela had to deal with personal issues as well as governmental. Mandela's decision to formally separate from Winnie in 1992 had taken a toll on him. Many of his friends had witnessed the pain he suffered in making the decision. In 1995, Mandela began divorce proceedings. The Mandelas' court appearance to finalize their divorce was emotional and sad. But Mandela knew that it was the right thing to do.[6]

Mandela met Graca Machel first in 1990, and then again in 1992, soon after he and his wife had separated. It was not long before he began to see her every chance he had. She was a strong, well-educated woman, the former minister for education and culture in Mozambique. She was the widow of the president of Mozambique, who had died in a plane crash in 1986. She had been a political activist and a teacher, and she had worked for the rights of women and children. In 1994, the Secretary General of the United Nations appointed her to complete an investigation and report on the impact of armed conflict on children. She presented the report in 1996, and it is responsible for improving the UN's policies regarding children who are caught up in war and conflict.

Thabo Mbeki (1942–)

Thabo Mbeki is the son of Govan Mbeki, who served on Robben Island with Nelson Mandela and others. Mbeki became chair of the ANC in 1989 and played an important role in the constitutional talks with the government that led to the free elections of 1994. He replaced Mandela as ANC president in 1997, and then succeeded him as president of South Africa in 1999. Mbeki was elected to a second term in 2004. After continued poverty in South Africa and unhappiness with his leadership, Mbeki lost his position as chair of the ANC to Jacob Zuma in 2007. Zuma was dismissed as Mbeki's deputy president in 2005 after being implicated in a corruption case. However, in 2008 a judge suggested that the prosecution of Zuma had been influenced by Mbeki's government. Mbeki denied the accusations, but the ANC called for him to resign, which he did in September 2008. Kgalema Motlanthe served as acting president leading up to the 2009 elections.

After his divorce was final in 1996, he and Graca began to be seen in public together. At first, some people had problems with the relationship. His ex-wife was still well liked among the youth, and people did not seem ready to see Mandela with another woman. Graca felt strong loyalty to her country of Mozambique. It was going through turmoil, and she did not want to leave it yet. Friends were glad to see Mandela happy and more relaxed, and many of his friends encouraged them to marry. They were finally married on Mandela's 80th birthday in 1998.[7]

TRANSFER OF POWER

In 1997, Mandela announced that he would not seek a second term and would retire from office in 1999. This left the door open for leadership of the country to be passed to the president of the ANC and Mandela's deputy vice president, Thabo Mbeki. Mbeki was different from Mandela in many ways. He was more of an academic, and some thought he lacked the friendly touch of Mandela. However, Mbeki had devoted his life to the ANC. He had been involved in political activism since age 14, and was the son of Govan Mbeki, an ANC leader who spent 24 years imprisoned at Robben Island. Mandela felt that Mbeki was the best person to succeed him. ❖

HEADLINES: 2000–2009

Here are some major news stories from the time of Mandela's retirement from politics.

Terrorists attack United States

On 11 September 2001, hijackers crashed commercial aeroplanes into the World Trade Center in New York City and the Pentagon building in Washington DC. A fourth hijacked plane crashed outside of Pittsburgh, presumed to have another target in mind. Nearly 3,000 people were killed. Islamic militant Osama bin Laden and the al Qaeda terrorist network were identified as the perpetrators. At the time, they were being sheltered in Afghanistan by the extremist Taliban government. In response, U.S. and British forces launched a military campaign against the Taliban government and al Qaeda terrorist camps in Afghanistan.

UK and U.S. launch war in Iraq

On 20 March 2003, the United Kingdom and the United States, with support from Australia, Spain, Poland, and Denmark, invaded Iraq. According to U.S. President George W. Bush and British Prime Minister Tony Blair, there were three reasons for the invasion: to disarm Iraq of weapons of mass destruction (WMDs), to end Saddam Hussein's support for terrorism, and to free the Iraqi people. After the invasion, no weapons of mass destruction were found in Iraq, and the occupation of the country became increasingly unpopular, both among Iraqis and UK and U.S. citizens.

Pluto downgraded

After arguing about Pluto's status since the 1990s, the International Astronomical Union voted to reclassify Pluto. Pluto became a dwarf planet in 2006, which meant that there were now only eight planets in Earth's Solar System. Many astronomers disagreed with the vote.

Peace in Northern Ireland

Leaders of Northern Ireland, who had been warring for many years, met face-to-face for the first time in 2007. Gerry Adams, the leader of Sinn Fein, and Ian Paisley, the head of the Democratic Unionist Party, worked out an agreement for a power-sharing government, in order to bring peace to the country.

Obama elected president

Barack Obama was sworn in as the first African-American president in United States history on 20 January 2009.

Beside his wife, Michelle, Obama took the oath of office, which was administered by Chief Justice John Roberts of the U.S. Supreme Court.

An international hero

*Even though Mandela retired from politics, he did not slow down his work for human rights. He travelled often, meeting with other well-known people in the business and political worlds. With them, he discussed the world, its problems, and what needed to be done in order to solve them. His main focus was the AIDS **epidemic** that was sweeping through Africa.*

FIGHTING AIDS

Mandela travelled all over the world, speaking and urging people to join the fight against AIDS. He called on nations to pledge money to help them fight the disease in Africa. In 2003, he created a campaign to fight AIDS, called 46664, named for his prison number while on Robben Island. He knew that in order to fight AIDS, he needed to reach young people. He reached out to celebrities, such as Bono, to help bring young people's attention to the problem. The campaign organized concerts and other events in order to raise money for and awareness of the fight against AIDS. Some feel that Mandela did not do enough to fight AIDS during his presidency – that he did not acknowledge the disease or do anything to stop it. He may not have understood the gravity of the disease at the time.[1] However, after his presidency, he worked hard to make up for lost time.

In 2005, Mandela's 54-year-old son, Makgatho L. Mandela, died of AIDS. One of the problems in fighting AIDS in South Africa had always been that people were ashamed and embarrassed to discuss it, especially if they had it. Because of this, it was very hard to talk about it and to teach people how to prevent it. After the death of Makgatho, Mandela made a public announcement of his death. He said: "Let us give publicity to HIV/AIDS and not hide it, because the only way to make it appear like a normal illness like TB, like cancer, is always to come out and say somebody has died because of HIV/AIDS, and people will stop regarding it as something extraordinary."[2]

Nelson Mandela and Graca Machel arriving in London, in 1997.

In comparison: Zimbabwe

Zimbabwe is another country in Africa with a history of conflict. White settlers there had taken the land from the black population. Guerrilla armies eventually forced the white government to hold elections. However, there was no Nelson Mandela in Zimbabwe to guide events towards a larger vision and healing process. Instead, Robert Mugabe became president in 1980 and clung to power. His new government seized large, white-owned farms, with the goal of giving land to black Zimbabweans. However, this led to a sharp fall in production, and the country has experienced a shortage of food. Many Zimbabweans have had to survive on grain handouts. Mugabe himself said that he would not leave power until all land is in the hands of the majority black population. Hundreds of thousands of Zimbabweans have left the country, especially those with the professional skills needed for a successful economy.

The turn of events in Zimbabwe following its independence demonstrates how important Mandela's role was in making sure South Africa's transition to its new government occurred without disaster or retribution against those formerly in control. Finally, following months of discussion over a power-sharing agreement, Morgan Tsvangirai (an opposition party candidate) was sworn in as prime minister of Zimbabwe in February 2009. In a speech after his inauguration, he called for an end to human rights abuses and political violence, and pledged to do everything in his power to help suffering Zimbabweans.

REPRESENTATIVE OF PEACE

Another issue very important to Mandela after his presidency was working for peace in and among nations. In January 2000, he travelled to Burundi, an African nation that had been in the midst of civil war since 1993. He lectured the powerful leaders of the warring groups, telling them to stop the wars and violence and to "join the modern world."[3] He criticized the countries' leaders, saying they had taken too long to find peace. In 2001, he did succeed in making a deal that included power sharing from the fighting parties, but the fighting soon began again. He continued to speak out against war, including against U.S. President George W. Bush's decision to go to war with Iraq. He spoke out fiercely against this, accusing the United States of going to war simply for oil.[4]

"Where there is poverty and sickness…
where human beings are being oppressed,
there is more work to be done.
Our work is for freedom for all…"
— Nelson Mandela

MANDELA'S LEGACY

Nelson Mandela is seen as a symbolic figure in the fight for human rights. Because of this he has been given many awards, and there have been many tributes to him. In 2001 he and his wife began an organization called The Elders. The Elders is a group of 12 world leaders from all over the world who work to solve world issues such as conflict, climate change, and oppression.

In 2000, ten years after his release from prison, Mandela celebrated by opening a museum in his honour. The museum is near the village of his birth, Mvezo, and the region where he grew up, Qunu. The Bhunga, or council, building holds many gifts that were sent to Mandela after his release from prison. The gifts came from countries around the world. Mandela said that he wanted to share these gifts with all people of South Africa.

Mandela's legacy in South Africa, and as a worldwide symbol, cannot be underestimated. Without his unique experience, personality, and skills, the world would likely have seen a bloodbath in South Africa. His willingness to rise above his own suffering allowed Mandela to work closely with white colleagues and create a truly multi-racial cabinet as president. His experience in jail and in negotiations taught Mandela that people of all races can often be reassured by a handshake and a smile. Mandela seemed uniquely capable of rising above race, at the exact moment when South Africa most needed that in a new leader.

The Nelson Mandela Foundation

The Nelson Mandela Foundation was created in 1999, first to handle responses to requests for speeches and for his help. Then it grew to something larger, focusing on making the world a better place by furthering Mandela's core values. Their vision statement is: "The Nelson Mandela Foundation contributes to the making of a just society by promoting the vision, values, and work of its Founder and convening dialogue around critical social issues."[5]

Mandela's is a case of one person with a larger-than-life personality moulding history in a positive way at a crucial moment. South Africa has many problems, and much work still needs to be done. All South Africans now enjoy freedom, but they do not yet all share prosperity. Narrowing the gap between rich and poor in South Africa is an ongoing challenge, among others. However, Mandela's legacy carries on, and he still speaks of a better future whenever he gets the chance, offering encouragement for those continuing the fight towards healing and progress.

In 2008, on Mandela's 90th birthday, a tribute concert was organized by his campaign, 46664. Many of the world's biggest stars came out to perform for the crowd, in celebration of Mandela's 90th birthday and to raise money and awareness for the AIDS crisis. Mandela acknowledged that there is still work to be done and improvements to be made, not

Nelson Mandela, at his 90th birthday celebration in London. To his right is UK Prime Minister Gordon Brown, and to his left is former U.S. President Bill Clinton.

just in South Africa but the rest of the world. He encouraged the next generation to carry on the work for a better world. In his short address to the crowd, Mandela said: "As we celebrate, let us remind ourselves that our work is far from complete. Where there is poverty and sickness, including AIDS, where human beings are being oppressed, there is more work to be done. Our work is for freedom for all … We say tonight, after nearly 90 years of life, it is time for new hands to lift the burdens. It is in your hands now, I thank you."[6] ❖

Timeline

1909	SOUTH AFRICA ACT PASSED BY BRITISH PARLIAMENT.
1910	AFTER THE SOUTH AFRICA ACT, THE UNION OF SOUTH AFRICA IS DECLARED AND INCLUDES THE FORMER BRITISH COLONIES OF THE CAPE AND NATAL, AND THE BOER REPUBLICS OF TRANSVAAL AND ORANGE FREE STATE.
1912	NATIVE NATIONAL CONGRESS FOUNDED, LATER RENAMED THE AFRICAN NATIONAL CONGRESS (ANC).
1914	NATIONAL PARTY FOUNDED.
1914–1918	WORLD WAR I
1918	SECRET BROEDERBOND (BROTHERHOOD) ESTABLISHED TO ADVANCE THE AFRIKANER CAUSE.
	On 18 July Nelson Rolihlahla Mandela is born in the Eastern Cape of South Africa.
1919	Mandela's father, Hendry, has his land and title taken from him by the British.
	Mandela and his mother move to be closer to her family.
1923	NNC BECOMES THE AFRICAN NATIONAL CONGRESS (ANC).
1927	Mandela's father dies. Jongintaba Dalindyebo, acting chief of the Thembu clan, becomes guardian of the nine-year-old Mandela.
1939–1940	Mandela enters Fort Hare University and completes two years before leaving for Johannesburg to avoid a marriage arranged for him by Chief Jongintaba.
1939–1945	WORLD WAR II
1941–1943	Mandela meets Walter Sisulu, who becomes a lifelong friend. Sisulu introduces Mandela to a law firm, where he obtains a position. Mandela earns his degree, enrolls in law school, and joins the ANC.
1943	New ANC constitution drafted and approved.
1944	Congress Youth League (CYL) formed within ANC by, among others, Oliver Tambo, Walter Sisulu, and Nelson Mandela.
	Mandela marries Evelyn Mase.
1944–1946	ANTI-PASS CAMPAIGN
1946	AFRICAN MINE WORKERS' STRIKE
1948	POLICY OF APARTHEID (SEPARATENESS) ADOPTED WHEN NATIONAL PARTY (NP) TAKES POWER. THEY IMPLEMENT NEW LAWS SUPPORTING **RACIAL DISCRIMINATION**.
1949	PROHIBITION OF MIXED MARRIAGES ACT
	ANC Youth League drafts a Program of Action calling for mass strikes, boycotts, protests, and passive resistance against apartheid policies.
1950	ANC responds to government suppression with campaign of civil disobedience, led by Nelson Mandela.
1951	Mandela becomes national president of the ANC Youth League.

1952	DEFIANCE CAMPAIGN

Mandela is arrested in July and charged for violating the Suppression of Communism Act. He and other ANC members are found guilty, but the sentence of nine months imprisonment is suspended for two years.

Mandela is banned from attending meetings or gatherings.

Mandela and Oliver Tambo open a law office in downtown Johannesburg.

At the annual ANC conference, Mandela becomes its deputy president. He draws up a plan for the ANC to work underground – the M-Plan.

1954 NATIVES RESETTLEMENT ACT

1955 ANC Congress of the People presents the Freedom Charter, which supports the abolition of racial discrimination and oppression.

1956 Mandela is arrested along with over 150 other people and tried for high treason. The "Treason Trial" takes up most of Mandela's time over the next few years.

1957 Mandela and Evelyn are divorced, and their three children stay with her.

1958 Mandela marries Winnie Madikizela. Over the next few years, two daughters are born, Zenani and Zindzi.

HENDRIK FRENSCH VERWOERD BECOMES PRIME MINISTER.

1959 A FORMER ANC YOUTH LEAGUE MEMBER, ROBERT SOBUKWE, LAUNCHES THE PAN AFRICANIST CONGRESS (PAC).

1960 SHARPEVILLE MASSACRE ON 21 MARCH

ANC and PAC are banned.

Mandela is arrested. Oliver Tambo leaves the country to work for the ANC from exile.

1961 SOUTH AFRICA BECOMES A REPUBLIC.

Mandela and the other defendants in the Treason Trial are found not guilty.

Mandela heads ANC's new military wing, which launches a sabotage campaign.

Mandela escapes the country and travels in Africa and Europe.

1962 Returning to South Africa in March, Mandela is arrested, convicted, and sentenced to five years in prison. He is held on Robben Island.

1963 ORGANIZATION OF AFRICAN UNITY (OAU) IS FORMED.

1963–1964 Although already serving a sentence, Mandela is brought to trial again along with other ANC leaders in what is known as the Rivonia Trial.

1964 ANC leader Mandela is sentenced to life imprisonment and sent to Robben Island.

1964–1992 SOUTH AFRICA EXCLUDED FROM THE OLYMPICS DUE TO RACIAL DISCRIMINATION.

1966 PRIME MINISTER HENDRIK VERWOERD ASSASSINATED. JOHN VORSTER SUCCEEDS HIM.

1967 OLIVER TAMBO BECOMES ANC PRESIDENT.

1968–1969 Within a one-year period, Mandela's mother dies and his eldest son is killed in a car crash. Mandela is not allowed to attend the funerals.

1969 SOUTH AFRICAN STUDENTS ORGANIZATION (SASO) FORMED UNDER STEVE BIKO.

1972	FIRST BLACK PEOPLE'S CONVENTION (BPC) NATIONAL CONGRESS
1974	UN GENERAL ASSEMBLY VOTES TO SUSPEND SOUTH AFRICA, BUT THE ACTION IS NOT CONFIRMED BY THE SECURITY COUNCIL.
1975	CHIEF GATSHA BUTHELEZI OF KWAZULU REVIVES THE INKATHA FREEDOM PARTY.
1976	MORE THAN 600 ARE KILLED IN SOWETO UPRISING.
1977	STEVE BIKO DIES FOLLOWING POLICE BRUTALITY DURING INTERROGATION.
	Winnie Mandela is banished to Brandfort, a remote township. Her daughter Zindzi goes with her. Over the following years, Winnie spends over a year in jail and faces constant harassment from the police. She becomes more aggressive and militant in opposing white rule.
	VORSTER RESIGNS. P. W. BOTHA TAKES OVER AS PRIME MINISTER.
1980	In exile, Oliver Tambo and the ANC launch the "Release Mandela" campaign.
1982	After 18 years on Robben Island, Mandela is transferred to Pollsmoor Prison on the mainland.
1984	BISHOP DESMOND TUTU AWARDED NOBEL PEACE PRIZE.
1984–1989	TOWNSHIP REVOLT AND STATE OF EMERGENCY
1985	PRESIDENT BOTHA'S "RUBICON" SPEECH, IN WHICH HE REFUSES TO REFORM.
	SOUTH AFRICA'S CHURCH LEADERS TAKE UP THE ANTI-APARTHEID CAUSE, LED BY BISHOP DESMOND TUTU.
	ANTI-APARTHEID RALLIES AND PROTESTS TAKE PLACE AROUND THE WORLD.
1986	SOUTH AFRICAN GOVERNMENT DECLARES A STATE OF EMERGENCY.
	Secret talks begin in July between Mandela and the government.
1988	ANC's "Constitutional Guidelines for a Democratic South Africa" is published.
	"FREEDOMFEST" IS HELD OUTSIDE LONDON AND TELEVISED IN 60 COUNTRIES.
	Mandela is transferred to Victor Verster Prison.
	Winnie Mandela is implicated in the murder of a 13-year-old boy.
1989	F. W. DE KLERK SUCCEEDS P. W. BOTHA AS PRESIDENT AND BEGINS TO MAKE REFORMS.
	PUBLIC FACILITIES ARE DESEGREGATED. MANY ANC ACTIVISTS ARE FREED.
1990	The ANC is no longer banned, and Mandela is released after 27 years in prison.
	F. W. DE KLERK ENDS APARTHEID.
	INKATHA FREEDOM PARTY IS LAUNCHED.
1991	DE KLERK REPEALS REMAINING APARTHEID LAWS, INTERNATIONAL SANCTIONS ARE LIFTED.
	There is major fighting between the ANC and Zulu Inkatha movement.
	Winnie's trial begins for kidnapping and assault. She is sentenced to six years in prison. In her appeal she is given a suspended sentence and fined.
	In July, the ANC holds its annual conference in South Africa for the first time. Mandela is elected ANC president.
1991–1992	CONVENTION FOR A DEMOCRATIC SOUTH AFRICA (CODESA) TAKES PLACE.
1992	In April, Mandela announces his separation from Winnie.
	Frustrated over the unsuccessful negotiations, the ANC decides on a policy of "rolling mass action" consisting of strikes, protests, and boycotts, to demonstrate the support the ANC has across the country.

Violence continues, with frequent clashes between police and residents.

Mandela says the police are supporting the violence. De Klerk says he does not have the power to control it.

The increasing death toll forces Mandela and de Klerk to restart negotiations in September. They sign the Record of Understanding, which promises to establish formal investigations into the violence and police actions. It also establishes an elected constitutional assembly that will develop a new constitution for the country.

1993	Parties agree on interim constitution.

In April, Chris Hani, a popular young ANC leader, is killed by a white extremist. Mandela appears on television calling for restraint and successfully prevents further violence.

Mandela and de Klerk are jointly awarded the Nobel Peace Prize.

1994 Mandela is elected president.

A Government of National Unity is formed, South Africa's Commonwealth membership is restored, and remaining sanctions are lifted. South Africa takes its seat in the UN General Assembly after a 20-year absence.

1996 THE TRUTH AND RECONCILIATION COMMISSION, CHAIRED BY ARCHBISHOP DESMOND TUTU, BEGINS HEARINGS ON HUMAN RIGHTS CRIMES COMMITTED DURING THE APARTHEID ERA.

Mandela and Winnie are divorced in March.

1997 THABO MBEKI BECOMES PRESIDENT OF THE ANC.

1998 THE TRUTH AND RECONCILIATION COMMISSION REPORT BRANDS APARTHEID A CRIME AGAINST HUMANITY AND FINDS THE ANC ACCOUNTABLE FOR HUMAN RIGHTS ABUSES.

Mandela marries Graca Machel.

1999 THABO MBEKI TAKES OVER AS PRESIDENT.

2001 39 MULTI-NATIONAL PHARMACEUTICAL COMPANIES HALT A LEGAL BATTLE TO STOP SOUTH AFRICA FROM IMPORTING GENERIC AIDS DRUGS. THIS IS HAILED AS A VICTORY FOR INTERNATIONAL EFFORTS TO IMPORT CHEAPER DRUGS TO COMBAT THE VIRUS.

2003 Walter Sisulu dies close to age 91.

2004 Mandela retires from public life.

THABO MBEKI WINS A SECOND TERM AS PRESIDENT.

2005 Mandela announces that his son, Makgatho, has died of an HIV/AIDS-related illness.

2006 FORMER DEPUTY PRESIDENT JACOB ZUMA IS ACQUITTED OF RAPE CHARGES AND IS REINSTATED AS DEPUTY LEADER OF THE GOVERNING ANC.

CORRUPTION CHARGES AGAINST ZUMA ARE DISMISSED.

2007 On his 89th birthday, Mandela announces the formation of The Elders.

2008 Mandela's 90th birthday is celebrated across South Africa. A concert is also held in London in honour of his birthday.

PRESIDENT MBEKI RESIGNS. PARLIAMENT CHOOSES ANC DEPUTY LEADER KGALEMA MOTLANTHE AS PRESIDENT.

2009 ANC WINS APRIL GENERAL ELECTION. JACOB ZUMA IS SET TO SUCCEED MOTLANTHE AS PRESIDENT.

Glossary

acquitted to have fulfilled or be free from a debt or obligation

African National Congress (ANC) African liberation movement formed in 1912 and later a political party. The goal of the ANC was to bring all Africans together as one people to defend their rights and freedoms. Once apartheid was ending in the early 1990s, the ANC emerged as the primary political party of South Africa.

Afrikaner South African of European descent whose native language is Afrikaans, which is a language developed from 17th-century Dutch

Allies group of countries that are friendly towards one another. In World War II, the Allies included the British Empire, the United States, and the U.S.S.R. (Soviet Union), which were united against the Axis powers of Germany, Italy, and Japan.

amnesty pardon granted by a government or authority

ancestor person from whom another person is descended

anthem popular song identified with a culture, movement, or country

apartheid policy of segregation and discrimination against non-European groups in South Africa

baptized to be made part of the Christian Church by the ceremony of being sprinkled with or submerged in water

Bolshevik member of the Russian Social Democratic Workers' Party that seized power of the country in 1917

boycott to stop doing something as an expression of protest

cabinet group of people appointed by the head of state to lead parts of the government and act as advisers

camaraderie spirit of goodwill among friends

chasm great difference of views or interests

civic relating to the affairs of a city or its citizens

co-educational educating both sexes

colonial having to do with a colony, which is a land settlement that is largely controlled by another, often distant, nation

Commonwealth also called the Commonwealth of Nations, this is a voluntary association of independent states, most of which were formerly part of the British Empire. Commonwealth members agree to certain values and goals, such as free trade, the rule of law, and individual liberty, and co-operate to promote them around the world.

communism theory or system where property is owned collectively by all the people and labour is organized to benefit all members equally

conspiracy treacherous or illegal plan formulated in secret by two or more people

diplomatic relating to diplomacy, which is conduct of relations among nations by officials, or diplomats

epidemic rapid spread or increase of something, such as a disease

exile banishment from one's homeland

fascism system of government with central authority in a dictator, with the government controlling the economy and suppressing its opposition; also characterized by extreme nationalism and racism

hearing preliminary examination in a criminal procedure, before going to trial

heir person who inherits something from another

idolize regard with blind devotion

inauguration formal induction into office

liberal open to new ideas for progress

mentor wise and trusted counsellor and supporter, usually older than the student

Methodism evangelical Protestant Church founded in England in the 18th century characterized by active concern with social welfare and public morals

mission group of persons sent by a church to carry out religious work in other places, often including establishing a church, school, hospital, etc.

nationalize to bring under the control of a nation

National Party governing party of South Africa between 1948 and 1994, which disbanded in 2005. It drew its support mostly from white, Dutch Afrikaners and English whites and was responsible for the policy of apartheid.

parliamentary relating to a parliament, which is a law-making body of a government

passive resistance opposition to a government or law by the use of non-violent methods, also known as civil disobedience

persecuted pursued and harassed, or annoyed, repeatedly

prosecution government institution and act of pursuing criminal charges against a defendant

prostate gland organ in males at the base of the bladder that plays a role in the excretion of urine and semen

racial discrimination showing prejudice or bias against a person or people based on race

reconciliation being restored to a state of harmony or friendship

regent ruler or governor

revolutionary person involved in a revolution, or radical change

rural related to the country and country life, as opposed to a city

sabotage destruction of property or prevention of a normal operation, or the act of doing those things

safe house dwelling or building that is a safe place to hide and carry on activities for members of an organization

sanction penalty imposed by other nations for the violation of a moral principle or international law

segregation practice of separating people of different races or classes. This practice almost always results in a particular group being given unfair privileges.

Sotho group of related Bantu languages spoken in southern Africa

strike purposeful stopping of work to achieve an aim for the workers

Transvaal region of northeast South Africa inhabited by Bantu-speaking black Africans and later settled by Boer farmers

United Party South Africa's ruling party between 1934 and 1948, which drew support from English-speakers, Afrikaners, and "coloureds," which include Africans who are not black or white. The United Party lost to the National Party in the 1948 election, which brought apartheid government.

Notes on sources

LEADER OF A RAINBOW NATION (PAGES 6-9)

1. Francis X. Clines, "The South African Vote: The Scene A Joyous Day of Lining Up to Vote for Many, but Disappointment for Some; Blacks and Whites, Waiting Together". *New York Times*, April 28, 1994, http://query.nytimes.com/gst/fullpage.html?res=9C06EEDD1730 F93BA15757C0A962958260.

2. Nelson Mandela, *Nelson Mandela: In His Own Words* (New York: Little, Brown and Company, 2003), 69.

ROLIHLAHLA (PAGES 12-27)

1. Anthony Sampson, *Mandela: The Authorized Biography* (New York: Alfred A. Knopf, 1999.), 192.

2. Mandela, *Nelson Mandela: In His Own Words,* 46–47.

3. Kofi Annan, Foreword, *Nelson Mandela: In His Own Words*, xiii.

4. Sampson, *Mandela: The Authorized Biography*, 6–7.

5. Mandela, *Nelson Mandela: In His Own Words*, 88.

6. Sampson, *Mandela: The Authorized Biography*, 8–9.

7. Sampson, *Mandela: The Authorized Biography*, 10.

8. Sampson, *Mandela: The Authorized Biography*, 10–11.

9. Sampson, *Mandela: The Authorized Biography*, 10.

10. As quoted from an unpublished jail memoir in Sampson, *Mandela: The Authorized Biography*, 11.

11. Chief Anderson Joyi, from "The Long Walk of Nelson Mandela", produced by *Frontline* for PBS, retrieved 3 March 2009, from http://www.pbs.org/wgbh/pages/frontline/ shows/mandela/interviews/chiefs.html.

12. Sampson, *Mandela: The Authorized Biography*, 16.

13. Sampson, *Mandela: The Authorized Biography*, 21.

14. Sampson, *Mandela: The Authorized Biography*, 36.

SPEAKING OUT (PAGES 30-43)

1. Nelson Mandela, *Mandela: An Illustrated Autobiography* (New York: Little, Brown and Company, 1996), 40.

2. Bruce W. Nelan and Peter Hawthorne, "Making Their Own Miracles", *TIME*, December 19, 1994, http://www.time.com/time/magazine/article/0,9171,982015-1,00.html.

3. Bill Keller, *Tree Shaker: The Story of Nelson Mandela* (Boston: Kingfisher, 2008), 40.

4. Sampson, *Mandela: The Authorized Biography*, 69.

5. Nelson Mandela, "People Are Destroyed" (October 1955), *The Struggle Is My Life* (New York: Pathfinder Press, 1986), 59.

6. Sampson, *Mandela: The Authorized Biography*, 68.

7. Oliver Tambo, Introduction to Nelson Mandela, *No Easy Walk to Freedom* (Portsmouth, NH: Heinemann, 1989), xi.

8. Nelson Mandela, *Long Walk to Freedom: The Autobiography of Nelson Mandela* (New York: Little, Brown and Company, 1994), 184.

9. Sampson, *Mandela: The Authorized Biography*, 88–92.

10. Adelaide Tambo, from "The Long Walk of Nelson Mandela", produced by *Frontline* for PBS, retrieved 3 March 2009, from http://www.pbs.org/wgbh/pages/frontline/shows/mandela/interviews/tambo.html.

11. Sampson, *Mandela: The Authorized Biography*, 304–305.

12. The Freedom Charter, Adopted at the Congress of the People, Kliptown, on June 26, 1955, retrieved 3 March 2009, from http://www.anc.org.za/ancdocs/history/charter.html.

13. Keller, *Tree Shaker*, 42.

14. Nelson Mandela, *The Struggle Is My Life* (New York: Pathfinder Press, 1986), 92.

15. Sampson, *Mandela: The Authorized Biography*, 147.

16. Manifesto of Umkhonto we Sizwe, Leaflet issued December 16, 1961, by the Command of Umkhonto we Sizwe, retrieved 3 March 2009, from http://www.anc.org.za/ancdocs/history/manifesto-mk.html.

PRISONER 46664 (PAGES 46-59)

1. Sampson, *Mandela: The Authorized Biography*, 154–155.

2. Sampson, *Mandela: The Authorized Biography*, 159.

3. Sampson, *Mandela: The Authorized Biography*, 170–171.

4. Keller, *Tree Shaker*, 44.

5. Mandela, *The Struggle Is My Life*, 181.

6. Keller, *Tree Shaker*, 48.

7. Mandela, *Long Walk to Freedom*, 394.

8. Keller, *Tree Shaker*, 51.

9. Keller, *Tree Shaker*, 52.

10. Sampson, *Mandela: The Authorized Biography*, 251.

11. Neville Alexander, from "The Long Walk of Nelson Mandela", produced by *Frontline* for PBS, retrieved 3 March 2009, from http://www.pbs.org/wgbh/pages/frontline/shows/mandela/interviews/alexander.html.

12. Sampson, *Mandela: The Authorized Biography*, 248.

13. Mandela, *The Struggle Is My Life*, 195–196.

A FREE MAN (PAGES 62-73)

1. Sampson, *Mandela: The Authorized Biography*, 378.

2. Mandela, *Mandela: An Illustrated Autobiography*, 171.

3. Sampson, *Mandela: The Authorized Biography*, 374.

4. Sampson, *Mandela: The Authorized Biography*, 393.

5. Sampson, *Mandela: The Authorized Biography*, 394.

6. Mandela, *Long Walk to Freedom*, 563.

7. Mandela, *Long Walk to Freedom*, 562–563.

8. Mandela, *Long Walk to Freedom*, 568.

9. Sampson, *Mandela: The Authorized Biography*, 403–404.

10. Sampson, *Mandela: The Authorized Biography*, 446–447.

PRESIDENT OF A NEW SOUTH AFRICA
(PAGES 76-85)

1. Nelson Mandela, *Nelson Mandela Speaks: Forging a Democratic, Nonracial South Africa* (New York: Pathfinder Press, 1993), 252.

2. Nelson Mandela, "Opening Address to the Third Session of Parliament", Cape Town, 9 February 1996, retrieved 3 March 2009, from http://www.info.gov.za/speeches/1996/f120r355.htm.

3. Sampson, *Mandela: The Authorized Biography*, 521.

4. Truth and Reconciliation Commission of South Africa Report, 21 March 2003, http://www.info.gov.za/otherdocs/2003/trc/.

5. Sampson, *Mandela: The Authorized Biography*, 525.

6. Sampson, *Mandela: The Authorized Biography*, 491–493.

7. Sampson, *Mandela: The Authorized Biography*, 541.

AN INTERNATIONAL HERO (PAGES 88-93)

1. Michael Wines, "Mandela, Anti-AIDS Crusader, Says Son Died of Disease", *New York Times,* 7 January 2005, http://www.nytimes.com/2005/01/07/international/africa/07mandela.html?scp=1&sq=mandela%20AIDS%20presidency&st=cse.

2. Michael Wines, "Mandela, Anti-AIDS Crusader, Says Son Died of Disease", *New York Times,* 7 January 2005, http://www.nytimes.com/2005/01/07/international/africa/07mandela.html?scp=1&sq=mandela%20AIDS%20presidency&st=cse.

3. Nelson Mandela, "Warring Sides in Burundi Get a Scolding From Mandela", *New York Times,* 17 January 2000, http://query.nytimes.com/gst/fullpage.html?res=9B02E2DB1E3AF934A25752C0A9669C8B63&n=Top/Reference/Times%20Topics/People/M/Mandela,%20Nelson.

4. "Mandela Condemns US Stance on Iraq", BBC News, 30 January 2003, http://news.bbc.co.uk/2/hi/africa/2710181.stm.

5. Retrieved 3 March 2009, from http://www.nelsonmandela.org/index.php/foundation/vision-and-mission/.

6. Nelson Mandela, "Nelson Mandela Addresses Crowd at 46664 Concert", 27 June 2008, http://www.nelsonmandela.org/index.php/news/article/nelson_mandela_addresses_crowd_at_46664_concert/.

Bibliography

ANC. The Freedom Charter, Adopted at the Congress of the People, Kliptown, on 26 June 1955. Retrieved 3 March 2009, from http://www.anc.org.za/ancdocs/history/charter.html.

BBC. "Mandela Condemns US Stance on Iraq". BBC News, 30 January 2003, http://news.bbc.co.uk/2/hi/africa/2710181.stm.

Clines, Francis X. "The South African Vote: The Scene A Joyous Day of Lining Up to Vote for Many, but Disappointment for Some; Blacks and Whites, Waiting Together". *New York Times*, 28 April 1994, http://query.nytimes.com/gst/fullpage.html?res=9C06EEDD1730F93 BA15757C0A962958260.

Keller, Bill. *Tree Shaker: The Story of Nelson Mandela*. Boston: Kingfisher, 2008.

Mandela, Nelson. *Long Walk to Freedom: The Autobiography of Nelson Mandela*. New York: Little, Brown and Company, 1994.

Mandela, Nelson. *Mandela: An Illustrated Autobiography*. New York: Little, Brown and Company, 1996.

Mandela, Nelson. "Nelson Mandela Addresses Crowd at 46664 Concert", 27 June 2008. Nelson Mandela Foundation, http://www.nelsonmandela.org/index.php/news/article/nelson_mandela_addresses_crowd_at_46664_concert/.

Mandela, Nelson. *Nelson Mandela: In His Own Words*. New York: Little, Brown and Company, 2003.

Mandela, Nelson. *Nelson Mandela Speaks: Forging a Democratic, Nonracial South Africa*. New York: Pathfinder Press, 1993.

Mandela, Nelson. *No Easy Walk to Freedom*. Portsmouth, NH: Heinemann, 1989.

Mandela, Nelson. "Opening Address to the Third Session of Parliament", Cape Town, 9 February 1996. Retrieved 3 March 2009, from http://www.info.gov.za/speeches/1996/f120r355.htm.

Mandela, Nelson. *The Struggle Is My Life*. New York: Pathfinder Press, 1986.

Mandela, Nelson. "Warring Sides in Burundi Get a Scolding From Mandela". *New York Times*, 17 January 2000, http://query.nytimes. com/gst/fullpage.html?res=9B02E2DB1E3AF934A25752C0 A9669C8B63&n=Top/Reference/Times%20Topics/People/M/ Mandela,%20Nelson.

Nelan, Bruce W., and Peter Hawthorne. "Making Their Own Miracles". *TIME*, 19 December 1994, http://www.time.com/time/magazine/ article/0,9171,982015-1,00.html.

Sampson, Anthony. *Mandela: The Authorized Biography*. New York: Alfred A. Knopf, 1999.

The Nelson Mandela Organisation. "Vision and Mission". Retrieved 3 March 2009, from http://www.nelsonmandela.org/index.php/ foundation/vision-and-mission/.

Truth and Reconciliation Commission. Truth and Reconciliation Commission of South Africa Report, 21 March 2003, http://www. info.gov.za/otherdocs/2003/trc/.

Umkhonto we Sizwe. "Manifesto of Umkhonto we Sizwe," Leaflet issued 16 December 1961, by the Command of Umkhonto we Sizwe. Retrieved 3 March 2009, from http://www.anc.org.za/ancdocs/history/ manifesto-mk.html.

WGBH Educational Foundation. "The Long Walk of Nelson Mandela". Produced by *Frontline* for PBS. Retrieved 3 March 2009, from http:// www.pbs.org/wgbh/pages/frontline/shows/mandela/interviews/chiefs. html.

Wines, Michael. "Mandela, Anti-AIDS Crusader, Says Son Died of Disease". *New York Times*, 7 January 2005, http://www.nytimes. com/2005/01/07/international/africa/07mandela.html?scp=1&sq=man dela%20AIDS%20presidency&st=cse.

Find out more

BOOKS

Beecroft, Simon. *Days That Changed the World: The Release of Nelson Mandela*. Milwaukee, WI: World Almanac Library, 2004.

Downing, David. *Witness to History: Apartheid in South Africa*. Oxford: Heinemann Library, 2004.

Joffe, Joel. *The State Vs. Nelson Mandela: The Trial That Changed South Africa*. Oxford: Oneworld Publications, 2007.

Keller, Bill. *Tree Shaker: The Story of Nelson Mandela*. London: Kingfisher, 2008.

Kramer, Ann. *Mandela: The Rebel Who Led His Nation to Freedom*. Washington, DC: National Geographic, 2005.

Mandela, Nelson. *Long Walk to Freedom: The Autobiography of Nelson Mandela*. London: Little, Brown and Company, 1994.

Mandela, Nelson. *Mandela: An Illustrated Autobiography*. London: Little, Brown and Company, 1996.

Mandela, Nelson. *Nelson Mandela: In His Own Words: From Freedom to Future*. London: Little, Brown and Company, 2004.

Mandela, Nelson. *Nelson Mandela Speaks: Forging a Democratic, Nonracial South Africa*. New York: Pathfinder Press, 1993.

Mandela, Nelson. *The Struggle Is My Life*. New York: Pathfinder Press, 1986.

Meredith, Martin. *Nelson Mandela: A Biography*. New York: St. Martin's Press, 1998.

Sampson, Anthony. *Mandela: The Authorized Biography*. London: HarperCollins, 2000

DVDS

The Long Walk of Nelson Mandela, produced by Frontline for U.S. television channel PBS, is a great source, with interviews of many people who have known Mandela during his life. You may be able to ask for a copy of the DVD for this television special at your local library. If it is unavailable, however, pictures, interviews, and a transcript of the show are available on the PBS website: http://www.pbs.org/wgbh/pages/frontline/shows/mandela/

Nelson Mandela. 2008
A detailed portrait of Mandela's fight against racial segregation.

Mandela – Son of Africa, Father of a Nation. 2007.
This documentary follows Mandela's life up to and beyond his release from prison.

Mandela. 1996.
Documentary that discusses Mandela's life, from birth to political leader. It features interviews with Mandela and his friends and colleagues. It also features newsreel footage of the turbulent past of Mandela and South Africa.

Great Souls: Nelson Mandela. 1996.
Part of the *Great Souls* series, this film documents the life of Nelson Mandela.

Mandela's Fight for Freedom. 1995.
This two-part documentary from the Discovery Channel chronicles Mandela's life and struggles.

Nelson Mandela: Free at Last. 1990.
This programme chronicles the life of Nelson Mandela. It includes interviews with friends, family, and prison guards.

WEBSITES

The Long Walk of Nelson Mandela

www.pbs.org/wgbh/pages/frontline/shows/mandela/

A summary of the television special The Long Walk of Nelson Mandela. *Includes interviews of people who have known Mandela at the various stages of his life, and their accounts of the man.*

Nelson Mandela Museum

www.nelsonmandelamuseum.org.za/index2.htm

Has pictures of Mandela's childhood villages and provides some background.

Robben Island Prison

www.robben-island.org.za

Includes information about the island, including pictures and maps.

South African History Online

http://www.sahistory.org.za/pages/index/menu.htm

South African History Online (SAHO) is a non-partisan, non-profit history project established in 2000 to address biases found in South African educational and cultural institutions. It has become an online encyclopedia of South African history and is full of useful information.

South Africa Information

http://www.info.gov.za/

South African government information, including links to past speeches.

Truth and Reconciliation Commission

http://www.doj.gov.za/trc/

Truth and Reconciliation Commission website.

Nelson Mandela Foundation

http://www.nelsonmandela.org/

The Nelson Mandela Foundation website.

Index